Super Simple
Air Fryer Chicken

60 Quick and Tasty Recipes

quadrille

Kate Calder

Photography by Ant Duncan

CONTENTS

Introduction

Whether you're a recent convert or a long-time evangelist, the air fryer revolution has now guaranteed this magical machine has a permanent place in our kitchens. We all know and bang on about the benefits of air frying, the speed, the savings, the convenience, the crispiness, the superior taste, but one thing we don't celebrate enough is the versatility it offers. With this book I hope to show you how limitless and exciting the options are with air frying, all based around just one central ingredient, the humble chicken! This much-loved meat is straightforward and adaptable because it's capable of taking on a huge number of flavour combinations; many of which are covered within this book.

On top of this, every single one of these sixty recipes requires no kettle, no hob, no oven, no grill, no microwave – just the ingredients, your air fryer basket and a big appetite. From weekend takeaway hacks to delicious midweek salads, and sharing platters to pastries, I hope this book inspires you to broaden your air frying repertoire and unlock the machine's full potential.

TIPS AND TRICKS

How does it work?
The simple science behind the air fryer is that the food cooks by hot air circulating around it, and using very little oil to do so.

Which model to buy?
There are many on the market, varying in price and size. I have written and tested these recipes using an affordable air fryer, as you don't require any fancy modes or gadgets, just ideally a fryer that has a basket (or baskets) with handles. This will give you easier access and allow you to shake and move the food around to get an even cook.

Don't crowd the basket
The hot air needs to be able to reach the food in order to cook it. Giving the basket a shake is common practice with an air fryer; the equivalent to stirring your sauce in a pan on the hob.

Adding the chicken in a single layer
When cooking chicken you will need to make sure it is added to the air fryer in a single layer to allow the hot air to reach all sides of it. In most of the recipes you will need to turn the pieces of chicken over. This ensures the chicken is being cooked through as well as speeding up the overall cooking time.
I prefer using a fork in each hand to flip my chicken. Tongs can be used but the grip can often slip, breaking the perfect crunchy batter. Forks give more control over the ingredients.

Interrupting the air fryer in the middle of cooking is never a problem
All machines have some form of pause button allowing you to access the basket, stopping the hot air blowing so you can tend to your dish as required.

Baking parchment and liners.
I use both homemade baking parchment liners for my basket as well as slightly fancier ones, which are easily found online. These are helpful when you want to have less mess and/or contain the cooking juices and prevent sticking. The only thing to watch out for is making sure to weigh the liner down. The circulating air can blow a loose corner of a liner on top of your food, which can interfere with the cooking process and lead to uneven results. Either cut the liner to the size you need or make sure you have food weighing down all corners and sides.

Cooking spray oil
Always used in healthy cooking recipes, it is only 1 calorie a spray and perfect for the air fryer, which requires very little oil to cook. Cooking spray oil is especially vital when recreating

anything with a batter; air fryers love a dry batter sprayed with oil. Many have tried but wet batters do not work in the air fryer! They don't have the deep-fry oil to keep them in place and make an unimaginable mess.

Which mode?

Most air fryers have multiple cooking functions on offer. To keep it simple, every recipe in this book only uses the basic air fry button. This allows you to change the temperature and timings you need. Some recipes call for a dual basket air fryer where others use one large 7.5 litre (8 quart) basket. Most of the recipes can be cooked in both types, maybe except for a round pie! (Some air fryers now have dual baskets where the barrier can be removed to make one large basket. Very handy indeed!)

A lot of air fryers have a preheat function, I didn't use it in these recipes.

It's up to you, as long as the chicken is cooked at the end of cooking time. You can tell the chicken is cooked when the fibres are set and the meat no longer looks like jelly when you cut into it or the temperature has reached 74°C/165°F on a meat thermometer.

Keeping it simple.

The following recipes are accessible for any level of chef, easy to follow, with easy-to-find ingredients. A handful have longer lists of ingredients (often when I'm trying to crack some of the nations's favourite takeaways) but the use of them is always straightforward.

Nothing fancy.

All ingredients should be easy to find in your local shop if not already in your storecupboard at home. When not using cooking spray oil, I refer to cooking oil generically. This means whatever oil you have available, as long as it has a high burn temperature like sunflower or rapeseed (canola). Please leave extra virgin olive oil for dressings and dips!

Grill plates.

Air fryers with a handle have a grill plate in their basket that can be removed. You can cook with or without them. Grill plates are great but are best utilised for dishes without sauces. They put the crispy crunch in the dish that air fryers are renowned for and are more versatile than you might imagine. Many people seem to use them for fish fingers and oven chips but as you'll see in this book they're capable of so much more!

LIGHT LUNCH

Tarragon Chicken Omelette

/ **Serves 2** / **Ready in 15 minutes** /

Line the air fryer's grill plate with a large piece of baking parchment so that the paper comes up the four sides about 3–4 cm (1¼–1½ in) high. I used a loaf tin (pan) liner.

Pour the eggs into the lined air fryer basket. Sprinkle over the salt, chicken, tarragon, Cheddar and then the shallot. Spray with oil. Cook at 190°C (375°F) for 10–12 minutes, depending on the size of your air fryer. The larger the width of your omelette the quicker the cooking time.

To check if your omelette is cooked, give the basket's handle a shake and if there's any wobble then the omelette needs a couple more minutes. The omelette is finished cooking when it is golden and there is no longer any wobble when shaken.

Carefully remove the baking parchment with the omelette in it from the basket by tipping the basket to one side and sliding it out onto a chopping board. Cut in half and share with a friend.

3 eggs, beaten
pinch of salt
1 cooked chicken breast, cut into bite-size pieces
2 tablespoons roughly chopped tarragon leaves (basil, parsley or dill would also work well)
handful of grated Cheddar
1 shallot, halved and finely sliced
cooking oil spray

This recipe works best in a single basket of a dual basket air fryer. If you have a large single air fryer, then add one more egg to the recipe.

Chicken Piccanta

Add the egg to a wide, shallow bowl or plate. In another bowl, mix the flour with the lemon zest, the salt and a few grinds of pepper. Spread this out onto a plate.

Add the chicken slices to the egg, turning them over a couple of times so the pieces are fully drenched. Lay the pieces flat in the flour, turning over a couple of times until coated.

Remove the grill plate from the air fryer. Spray the basket with oil, then add the chicken in a single layer and spray all over with oil. Cook at 200°C (400°F) for 10 minutes, turning the pieces over halfway through cooking.

Meanwhile, in a measuring jug, mix the chicken stock with the lemon juice, capers, garlic, salt and parsley.

Add the caper sauce to the basket. Turn the chicken over a couple of times to get saucy and cook again at 200°C (400°F) for 5 minutes.

Divide the chicken between serving plates and spoon over the sauce. Serve with crusty bread to mop up the juices.

1 egg, beaten
3 tablespoons plain (all-purpose) flour
zest and juice of 1 lemon
pinch of salt
freshly ground black pepper
2 skinless chicken breasts, cut into 1 cm (½ in) slices widthways
cooking oil spray
crusty bread, to serve

FOR THE SAUCE
120 ml (4 fl oz/½ cup) ready-made chicken stock
2 tablespoons capers
1 garlic clove, crushed
pinch of salt
2 tablespoons chopped flat leaf parsley

Summer Veg, Chicken and Rice with a Herby Dressing

/ Serves 2 / Ready in 30 minutes /

Mix the rice, herbs, lemon zest and garlic together in a large bowl.

Remove the air fryer's grill plate, then add the rice mixture to the basket. On top of the rice mixture, add the chicken, cherry tomatoes, red onion and courgette. Crumble over the feta in large chunks. Squeeze half of the lemon over everything, then sprinkle over the salt and a few grinds of pepper. Spray all over with oil and cook at 200°C (400°F) for 15 minutes, turning the chicken over halfway through cooking. The chicken is done when cooked through and the vegetables are starting to char.

Meanwhile, to make the dressing, in a small bowl, mix the finely chopped herbs with the olive oil. Squeeze in the juice from the other half of the lemon and add the salt and a grind of pepper. Stir everything together and set aside.

Serve the chicken, vegetables and rice with a drizzle of herby dressing on top.

photograph overleaf

250 g (9 oz) pouch microwave rice (I used Tilda Wholegrain Basmati & Wild Rice)
handful of basil leaves, sliced
handful of mint leaves, sliced
zest of 1 lemon, then halved
1 garlic clove, crushed
2 skinless, boneless chicken breasts
100 g (3½ oz) cherry tomatoes
1 small red onion, halved and sliced
1 courgette (zucchini), halved and sliced
½ x 200 g (7 oz) block of feta
2 pinches of salt
freshly ground black pepper
cooking oil spray

FOR THE HERBY DRESSING
handful of basil leaves, finely chopped
handful of mint leaves, finely chopped
2 tablespoons extra virgin olive oil
pinch of salt

Asparagus, Tomato and Chicken Tart

/ Serves 2 / Ready in 30 minutes /

Remove the grill plate from the air fryer and lay the pastry on top of it. Fold over any ends that are hanging off so the pastry sheet fits just inside the grill plate. Brush the pastry with the egg.

Replace the grill plate, with the pastry on it, in the basket and cook at 200°C (400°F) for 6 minutes.

Meanwhile, in a bowl, mix the crème fraîche with the lemon zest and a few grinds of pepper. In another bowl, mix the chicken with the garlic powder and mixed herbs.

Carefully turn the sheet of pastry over on the grill plate so the cooked side is now on the bottom. Leaving it on the grill plate, dollop over the crème fraîche mixture and gently spread all over leaving a small border. Add the chicken, asparagus and sundried tomatoes. Spray all over with oil and sprinkle with a pinch of salt. Cook at 200°C (400°F) for 8 minutes, or until the tart is golden and crisp.

Slice in half and serve.

½ x 320 g (11 oz) puff pastry sheet (I used Jus Rol)
1 egg, beaten
4 tablespoons crème fraîche
zest of 1 lemon
freshly ground black pepper
1 skinless, boneless chicken thigh, sliced
½ teaspoon garlic powder or granules
½ teaspoon dried mixed herbs
6 asparagus tips, woody ends removed
3 sundried tomatoes, halved
cooking oil spray
pinch of salt

Stuffed Peppers

/ Serves 2 / Ready in 30 minutes /

Mix the chicken, feta, tomatoes, olives, garlic, thyme, chilli flakes, oil, salt and a few grinds of pepper together in a large bowl.

Lay out the 4 pepper halves. Using a spoon, divide the chicken and feta mixture evenly between the peppers.

Line the air fryer's grill plate with baking parchment. Place the stuffed peppers in the basket in a single layer and cook at 180°C (350°F) for 18 minutes, or until the chicken is cooked through.

The peppers will be juicy so carefully remove them using tongs or two forks, and serve with a salad and/or crusty bread.

4 skinless, boneless chicken thighs, cut into chunks
½ x 200 g (7 oz) block of feta, crumbled
4 cherry tomatoes, halved
4 pitted kalamata olives
1 garlic clove, crushed
1 teaspoon thyme, fresh or dried
¼ teaspoon chilli (hot pepper) flakes
1 tablespoon cooking oil
large pinch of salt
freshly ground black pepper
2 red (bell) peppers, halved lengthways and seeded

Teriyaki Sushi Rolls

/ Serves 2 / Ready in 30 minutes /

Remove the grill plate from the air fryer's basket. Break up the block of rice into small pieces and add them to the basket. Sprinkle over the water and cook at 190°C (375°F) for 3 minutes. Set aside to cool.

Add the chicken to the air fryer's basket in a single layer (there's no need to wash the basket). Spray with oil and cook at 200°C (400°F) for 12 minutes, turning halfway through cooking.

Drizzle 1 tablespoon of the teriyaki sauce over the chicken and turn the pieces over a few times to coat. Close the air fryer and leave to heat through for 1 minute.

Remove the teriyaki chicken from the air fryer and slice each piece of chicken lengthways into 3 strips. There should be 9 strips of chicken in total.

Working with one roll at a time, lay out a nori sheet, rough side up. Slightly wet your hands with water and spread half of the rice evenly over the nori, leaving 1 cm (½ in) at the top bare.

Place half of the chicken down the centre of the rice, then repeat with the cucumber and avocado slices. Drizzle another tablespoon of teriyaki sauce over the filling and dampen the last 1 cm (½ in) of bare nori with water to help seal when rolled.

To roll, bring up the end and pull it over the filling and compress lightly. Roll again and compress, then repeat until finished. Repeat the filling and rolling with the second sheet of nori.

To slice, use a sharp knife and have a damp cloth ready to wipe the knife of sticky rice between slices. First, slice the ends off each roll, then continue to slice into about 8 even pieces.

Drizzle the pieces with the remaining teriyaki sauce and serve with soy sauce and wasabi mustard.

250 g (9 oz) pouch microwave ready-cooked sushi rice (I used Tilda Microwave Sticky Rice)
2 tablespoons water
1 small skinless, boneless chicken breast, sliced into 3 pieces lengthways
cooking oil spray
4 tablespoons teriyaki sauce
2 sheets of nori
½ (lengthways) cucumber, seeded and sliced into 6 long strips
½ avocado, halved, peeled and thinly sliced

TO SERVE
dark soy sauce
wasabi mustard

Orange Chicken, Avocado and Pine Nut Wrap

/ Serves 2 / Ready in 20 minutes /

Slice the chicken breast lengthways so it opens out like a book and continue to slice all the way through into 2 pieces.

Mix the chicken halves, orange zest, 1 tablespoon of the juice, the olive oil, salt and a few grinds of pepper together in a large bowl. Turn the chicken over a few times to get it well coated in the marinade.

Line the air fryer's grill plate with baking parchment. Arrange the chicken on the baking parchment and cook at 200°C (400°F) for 10 minutes, turning the chicken over halfway through cooking.

Meanwhile, in a large bowl, mix the mayonnaise with the salt, a few grinds of pepper and another tablespoon of orange juice. Add the sliced avocado and spinach and toss together.

Once the chicken is finished cooking, check it is done by cutting through and making sure the fibres are set.

Lay out the wraps side by side on a chopping board and divide the cooked chicken between them. Sprinkle the pine nuts over the chicken, then evenly divide the avocado and spinach salad between the wraps. Working with one wrap at a time, fold the ends in and roll up tightly.

Slice the wraps in half and serve.

1 skinless, boneless chicken breast
zest and juice of 1 orange
1 teaspoon extra virgin olive oil
pinch of salt
freshly ground black pepper
2 large flour tortilla wraps (I used Fitzgerald's)
2 teaspoons toasted pine nuts

FOR THE SALAD
2 tablespoons mayonnaise
pinch of salt
1 avocado, halved, pitted and sliced
2 handfuls of spinach

Crispy Sesame Chicken Salad

/ Serves 2 / Ready in 20 minutes /

Spread the flour out on a plate. Add the egg to a shallow wide bowl or plate, then pour the rice cereal into a shallow bowl or plate.

Coat the chicken pieces all over in the flour, then dip them into the egg, turning over a couple of times so they are fully drenched. Finally, coat the chicken in the cereal, turning over a few times until completely coated.

Remove the grill plate from the air fryer and spray the basket with oil. Add the chicken in a single layer and spray with oil. Cook at 190°C (375°F) for 9 minutes, turning over halfway through cooking.

For the sauce, in a bowl, mix all the ingredients together.

Pour the sauce onto the chicken and turn the pieces to coat every one. Cook at 190°C (375°F) for a further 3 minutes.

For the salad, in a large bowl, mix the olive oil with the lime juice, honey, sesame seeds and salt. Add the lettuce, spring onions and avocado and toss together.

Serve the crispy sesame chicken alongside the salad and enjoy.

1 tablespoon plain (all-purpose) flour
1 egg, beaten
50 g (1¾ oz) puff riced cereal (I used Rice Krispies)
1 skinless, boneless chicken breast, sliced
cooking oil spray

FOR THE SAUCE
1 teaspoon sesame oil
1 garlic clove, crushed
¼ teaspoon Chinese 5 spice
2 tablespoons light soy sauce
1 tablespoon sweet chilli sauce
2 tablespoons runny honey

FOR THE SALAD
1 tablespoon extra virgin olive oil
juice of 1 lime
1 teaspoon runny honey
1 teaspoon toasted sesame seeds
pinch of salt
1 little gem lettuce, leaves separated and roughly chopped
2 spring onions (scallions)
1 avocado, peeled, pitted and sliced

Smoky Chicken Quesadillas

/ Serves 2 / Ready in 30 minutes /

Mix the chicken strips, oil, smoked paprika, chilli flakes and salt together in a large bowl.

Line the air fryer's grill plate with baking parchment. Arrange the chicken in a single layer on the parchment and cook at 200°C (400°F) for 12 minutes, turning over halfway though cooking.

Meanwhile, lay the tortillas out side by side on a chopping board. Sprinkle a quarter of the cheese over half of the first tortilla and then the second. Add half of the spring onions, tomato and jalapeños to the first tortilla, then repeat with the second.

Check if the chicken is cooked through after the 12 minutes, then roughly slice it. Discard the used baking parchment. There's no need to clean the air fryer. Divide the sliced chicken between the tortillas.

Finish each tortilla with a sprinkling of the remaining cheese and fold the tortillas over into half-moons. Carefully transfer to the grill plate one by one, using both hands, so they sit side by side. Cook at 200°C (400°F) for 1 minute, then open the air fryer and press the quesadillas firmly down with a spatula to help seal them shut. Cook for a further 2 minutes, or until the tortillas are slightly golden and toasted.

Serve with your favourite hot sauce.

1 skinless, boneless chicken breast, cut lengthways into 3 strips
1 teaspoon cooking oil
1 teaspoon smoked paprika
¼ teaspoon chilli (hot pepper) flakes
pinch of salt
2 large flour tortillas
110 g (3½ oz) Cheddar, grated
2 spring onions (scallions), chopped
1 tomato, chopped
4 pickled jalapeño pepper slices, chopped
Hot sauce, to serve

Cranberry, Chicken and Brie with Crispy Shallots Baguette

/ Serves 1 / Ready in 20 minutes /

Mix the chicken, 1 tablespoon of the cranberry sauce, 1 tablespoon of the mayonnaise, the salt and a few grinds of pepper together in a large bowl.

Line the air fryer's grill plate with baking parchment. Arrange the chicken strips on the parchment in a single layer and cook at 200°C (400°F) for 12 minutes, turning the strips over halfway through cooking.

Once the chicken is cooked, add a slice of Brie to each strip of chicken and cook again for 1 minute at 200°C (400°F). Remove and set aside.

For the crispy shallots, discard the baking parchment from the air fryer and spray the grill plate with oil. Add the shallots in a single layer, spray with oil and sprinkle with the salt. Cook at 160°C (325°F) for 3 minutes. Give the basket a shake and cook for a further 3 minutes.

Spread the remaining tablespoon of mayonnaise and cranberry sauce along the bottom half of the baguette. Add the Brie-topped chicken, then sprinkle over the shallots. Add the watercress and top with the other half of the baguette.

Cut in half and enjoy.

1 skinless, boneless chicken breast, sliced lengthways into 3 strips
2 tablespoons whole cranberry sauce
2 tablespoons mayonnaise
pinch of salt
freshly ground black pepper
3 long slices Brie cheese

FOR THE SHALLOTS
cooking oil spray
1 shallot, thinly sliced and rings separated
pinch of salt

FOR THE BAGUETTE
1 small baguette/baguettine, cut in half lengthways
handful of watercress

If you have a dual basket air fryer, then cook the shallots at the same time as the chicken. If not, then cook the shallots after the chicken while the chicken is resting.

Hot Chicken and Coleslaw Wraps

/ Serves 2 / Ready in 15 minutes /

For the coleslaw, mix the cabbage, red onion, carrot, yoghurt, mayonnaise, vinegar, salt and a few grinds of pepper together in a large bowl.

Lay out the tortilla wraps on a chopping board. Spread a tablespoon of mayonnaise on each, then divide the chicken, jalapeños, cheese and coleslaw between the two. Fold one end of the tortilla over the mixture, then tuck in the sides. Continue to roll tightly all the way up. Repeat with the second wrap.

Add the wraps, seam-side down, to the air fryer's grill plate and cook at 200°C (400°F) for 5 minutes, or until lightly golden. Serve.

FOR THE COLESLAW
¼ small white cabbage, cored and thinly sliced
1 small red onion, thinly sliced
1 carrot, grated
3 tablespoons plain yoghurt
1 tablespoon mayonnaise
1 tablespoon white wine vinegar
large pinch of salt
freshly ground black pepper

FOR THE WRAPS
2 large flour tortilla wraps (I used Fitzgerald's)
2 tablespoons mayonnaise
1 cooked chicken breast, thinly sliced or 150 g (5½ oz) pack sliced cooked chicken
8–10 pickled jalapeño pepper slices, chopped
4 heaped tablespoons grated Cheddar

Crispy Chicken Panzanella Salad

/ Serves 4 / Ready in 30 minutes /

Spray the pieces of bread with oil and add to the air fryer's grill plate in a single layer. Cook at 200°C (400°F) for 4 minutes, or until golden. Remove and set aside.

Lay the chicken on the air fryer's grill plate, skin-side up. Spray with oil and sprinkle with 2 pinches of salt. Cook at 200°C (400°F) for 15 minutes, or until the chicken is cooked through and the skin is crisp and golden.

Cut the chicken into pieces a similar size to that of the toasted bread. Set aside.

In a large bowl, whisk the olive oil with the vinegar, garlic, mustard, a large pinch of salt and a few grinds of pepper. Add the tomatoes, toasted bread and chicken and toss together. Finish by folding in the basil and mozzarella. Serve.

4 slices (about 110 g/3½ oz)
  ciabatta or sourdough bread,
  cut into bite-size pieces
cooking oil spray
2 boneless chicken breasts,
  skin on
salt and freshly ground black
  pepper
2 tablespoons extra virgin olive oil
1 tablespoon red wine vinegar
1 garlic clove, crushed
1 teaspoon Dijon mustard
300 g (10½ oz) cherry tomatoes,
  halved
2 handfuls of basil leaves, big
  ones torn in half
1 Buffalo mozzarella ball, torn

DINNER FOR TWO

Chicken Kyiv

/ Serves 2 / Ready in 30 minutes, plus chilling /

Mix the butter, chopped parsley and garlic together in a small bowl until well combined. Pop it into the refrigerator or freezer to chill and firm up for 10 minutes.

Meanwhile, use a sharp knife to make a deep pocket in the side of each chicken breast. Be careful not to cut all the way through or the butter filling will escape when cooking.

Divide the chilled butter in half and shape into two equal balls. Push each ball into a pocket of the chicken, then press the palm of your hand on each breast to flatten and help seal the pocket.

Add the flour to a large plate and sprinkle over a large pinch of salt and a few grinds of pepper. Pour the beaten eggs into a shallow bowl. Add the breadcrumbs to a third plate and mix with the remaining large pinch of salt.

Coat each chicken breast first in the flour, then dip into the egg, coating it all over and finally, in the breadcrumbs until coated. Lay your coated chicken breasts on a plate and chill in the refrigerator for 30 minutes, then coat the chicken in the egg and breadcrumbs again.

Spray each chicken breast all over with oil. Lay them out in a single layer, not touching, on the air fryer's grill plate and cook at 200°C (400°F) for 5 minutes. Spray the breasts again with oil and continue cooking for a further 15 minutes, or until cooked through (if you have a meat thermometer it should read at least 74°C/165°F).

Leave to rest for 5 minutes before serving.

50 g (1¾ oz) salted butter, softened
handful of fresh parsley, finely chopped
2 garlic cloves, crushed
2 skinless, boneless chicken breasts
2 tablespoons plain (all-purpose) flour
2 large pinches of salt
freshly ground black pepper
2 eggs, beaten
75 g (2½ oz/1¼ cups) panko breadcrumbs
cooking oil spray

Chicken and Mushroom Stroganoff

/ Serves 2 / Ready in 30 minutes /

Mix the garlic, paprika and tomato ketchup together in a large bowl. Stir in the chicken. Cover and set aside.

Remove the air fryer's grill plate. Add the rice and water to the basket and cook at 200°C (400°F) for 2–4 minutes until cooked to your liking. Divide between two plates, loosely cover and set aside.

Add the oil, mushrooms and shallot to the air fryer's basket. Stir and cook at 200°C (400°F) for 8 minutes, stirring halfway through cooking.

Add the marinated chicken to the mushrooms and shallot. Stir everything together and cook at 200°C (400°F) for 6 minutes, stirring halfway through cooking. Add the soured cream, salt and a few grinds of pepper and cook for a further 2 minutes, stirring halfway through cooking.

Divide the stroganoff between the rice plates, sprinkle with parsley and serve.

1 garlic clove, crushed
1 tablespoon sweet smoked paprika
1 tablespoon tomato ketchup
4 skinless, boneless chicken thighs, sliced
250 g (9 oz) pouch microwave basmati rice (I used Tilda Pure Basmati Rice)
2 tablespoons water
1 tablespoon cooking oil
150 g (5½ oz) chestnut mushrooms, sliced
1 shallot, thinly sliced
150 ml (5 fl oz/scant ⅔ cup) sour cream
pinch of salt
freshly ground black pepper
handful of fresh parsley, chopped

If you have a dual basket air fryer, then cook the rice at the same time as the chicken and mushrooms.

Cashew Chicken

If you have a dual basket air fryer, then cook the rice at the same time as the chicken.

/ Serves 2 / Ready in 30 minutes /

Remove the air fryer's grill plate and add the cooking oil, broccoli, onion and chilli to the basket. Stir together and cook at 200°C (400°F) for 5 minutes, stirring halfway through cooking.

Add the chicken, cornflour, salt and white pepper to a large bowl and stir to combine.

In another bowl, make the sauce by mixing the garlic with the ginger, soy sauce, honey and sesame oil. Set aside.

Add the coated chicken and the sauce to the broccoli in the air fryer. Mix everything together well and cook at 200°C (400°F) for 10 minutes, stirring a couple of times during cooking.

Stir in the cashews and cook for a final 2 minutes. Divide the cashew chicken between two plates and set aside.

Add the rice to the basket (there's no need to clean the basket). Stir in the water and cook at 200°C (400°F) for 2 minutes.

Serve the cashew chicken with the rice and enjoy.

1 tablespoon cooking oil
200 g (7 oz) Tenderstem broccoli, halved
1 onion, finely sliced
1 red chilli, halved and sliced
4 skinless, boneless chicken thighs, sliced
1 tablespoon cornflour (cornstarch)
large pinch of salt
few shakes of ground white pepper
1 garlic clove, chopped
2 cm (¾ in) piece of fresh ginger, peeled and chopped
2 tablespoons dark soy sauce
1 tablespoon runny honey
1 teaspoon sesame oil
75 g (2½ oz/½ cup) raw cashew nuts

FOR THE RICE
250 g (9 oz) pouch microwave basmati rice (I used Tilda Pure Basmati Rice)
2 tablespoons water

Hot Honey Chicken with Sweet Potato Chips

/ Serves 2 / Ready in 30 minutes /

Using a sharp knife, slice the chicken breast horizontally so it opens out like a book, then continue to slice all the way through into two pieces. Set aside.

Crush the cornflakes in a bowl using the end of a rolling pin. Pour out onto a plate and set aside.

Spread the flour out on a large plate and mix with a large pinch of salt and a few grinds of pepper. Beat the egg and crushed garlic together in a bowl, then pour out into a shallow bowl.

Add the first piece of chicken to the seasoned flour and turn over a couple of times to dust all over. Then dip the chicken into the garlicky egg, turning over a few times until completely coated. Finally, add the chicken to the cornflakes, again turning over a few times until completely coated. Set aside and repeat with the second piece of chicken.

Spray the air fryer's grill plate with oil. Lay the two pieces of chicken out in a single layer and spray them all over with oil. Cook at 180°C (350°F) for 5 minutes. Turn the pieces over and cook for a further 4 minutes.

Meanwhile, to make the hot honey sauce, mix all the ingredients together in small bowl.

Spoon 2 teaspoons of the sauce over each piece of chicken and cook at 180°C (350°F) for 1 minute. Turn the chicken over and spoon over the remaining sauce. Cook for a further 1 minute and check to see if the chicken is done cooking by making a small cut and checking the fibres are set. Remove the chicken from the air fryer, cover lightly with kitchen foil and leave to rest.

Add the sweet potato chips to the air fryer (there's no need to clean it). Spray all over with oil and sprinkle with salt. Cook at 200°C (400°F) for 14 minutes, shaking the basket halfway through cooking.

Serve the hot honey chicken alongside the chips.

FOR THE CHICKEN
1 large skinless, boneless chicken breast
80 g (2¾ oz/2⅔ cups) cornflakes
2 tablespoons plain (all-purpose) flour
salt and freshly ground black pepper
1 egg
1 garlic clove, crushed
cooking oil spray

FOR THE HOT HONEY SAUCE
3 tablespoons runny honey
1 tablespoon hot sauce (I used Frank's Original)
½ teaspoon chilli (hot pepper) flakes
½ teaspoon cider vinegar

FOR THE CHIPS
2 sweet potatoes, peeled and cut into 1–2 cm (½–¾ in) thick chips
large pinch of salt

If you have a dual basket air fryer, then cook the chips at the same time as the chicken.

Harissa Squash and Chicken with Lemon and Herb Dressing

/ Serves 2 / Ready in 30 minutes /

Mix the squash, chicken, spring onions, oil, harissa and 1 tablespoon of the yoghurt together in a large bowl.

Line the air fryer's grill plate with baking parchment. Remove the spring onions from the mixture, then pour the squash and chicken mixture into the basket in a single layer. Cook at 200°C (400°F) for 10 minutes. Turn the squash and chicken pieces over and arrange the spring onions on top. Cook for a further 8 minutes and check to see if the chicken is cooked through by making a small cut and seeing if the fibres are set. It is okay if the chicken and vegetables are becoming charred; it's the flavour that you want.

Meanwhile, to make the dressing, mix the remaining yoghurt with the herbs, lemon juice, salt and a few grinds of pepper together in a bowl. Set aside.

Serve the harissa squash, chicken and spring onions with the dressing on the side or drizzled on top.

½ butternut squash, peeled, seeded and cut into 2 cm (¾ in) thick wedges
4 skinless, boneless chicken thighs
2 spring onions (scallions), cut into into 5 cm (2 in) pieces
1 teaspoon cooking oil
2 tablespoons harissa paste
4 tablespoons Greek yoghurt
handful of soft herbs, chopped (I used coriander/cilantro and basil)
juice of 1 lemon
large pinch of salt
freshly ground black pepper

Chicken Supreme with New Potatoes

/ Serves 2 / Ready in 30 minutes /

Remove the air fryer's grill plate. Add the potatoes and oil to the air fryer's basket and mix together to coat. Spread out in an even single layer and sprinkle with the salt. Cook at 200°C (400°F) for 12 minutes, shaking the basket halfway through cooking. Once they are golden and cooked through, remove the potatoes from the basket, loosely cover with kitchen foil and set aside.

For the chicken, add the oil, bacon, mushrooms, shallot and chicken breasts, skin-side down, to the air fryer's basket (there's no need to clean the basket) and cook at 200°C (400°F) for 5 minutes.

Stir the bacon, mushrooms and shallot and turn the chicken breasts over so they are now skin-side up. Add the garlic and wine and cook for a further 5 minutes.

Mix the mustard, stock cube and cream together in a bowl, then pour over the chicken and vegetables. Stir and cook again at 200°C (400°F) for 8 minutes, or until the chicken is golden and cooked through.

Using tongs, lift out the chicken breasts and divide them between serving plates. Stir the sauce, then pour the sauce evenly over the chicken. Sprinkle with parsley and serve with the potatoes.

FOR THE POTATOES
350 g (12 oz) baby new potatoes, large ones halved
2 teaspoons cooking oil
pinch of salt

FOR THE CHICKEN
1 tablespoon cooking oil
2 rashers of smoked bacon, sliced into 2 cm (¾ in) wide pieces
4 chestnut mushrooms, sliced
1 shallot, finely chopped
2 boneless chicken breasts, skin on
1 garlic clove, crushed
50 ml (1¾ fl oz/3½ tablespoons) white wine
2 teaspoons Dijon mustard
¼ chicken stock cube
100 ml (3½ fl oz/scant ½ cup) double (heavy) cream
handful of fresh parsley, chopped

If you have a dual basket air fryer, you can cook the potatoes at the same time as the chicken.

Chicken, Chorizo and Prawn Paella

/ Serves 2 / Ready in 40 minutes /

Mix the rice, saffron, smoked paprika and stock together in a large bowl, making sure to separate all the rice grains. Add the red pepper, spring onions, garlic and chorizo and stir again. Carefully pour the mixture into the pie dish or cake tin (pan) and spread out evenly.

Put the chicken thighs, skin-side up, side by side in the dish on top of the rice. Add the prawns around the chicken. Spray the dish with oil and season with the salt and a few grinds of pepper.

Cook at 180°C (350°F) for 22 minutes or until the chicken is cooked through – make a small cut and check to see if the fibres are set. Using oven gloves, remove the hot dish onto a chopping board using. Sprinkle with parsley and serve.

250 g (9 oz) pouch microwave long grain rice, squeeze pouch to break up the rice
small pinch of saffron strands
¼ teaspoon smoked paprika
200 ml (7 fl oz/scant 1 cup) ready-made chicken stock
1 roasted red (bell) pepper from a jar, chopped
4 spring onions (scallions), chopped
1 garlic clove, crushed
70 g (2½ oz) dry-cured chorizo sausage, sliced
6 raw king prawns (shrimp)
2 chicken thighs, with skin on and bones in
cooking oil spray
pinch of salt
freshly ground black pepper
handful of fresh parsley, chopped

You will need a round pie dish or cake tin (pan) that fits inside your air fryer's basket. I used a 20 cm (8 in) sandwich tin (pan) without a removable base.

Chicken, Apricot and Pistachio Tagine with Couscous

/ Serves 2 / Ready in 20 minutes /

Combine the ras-el-hanout spice mix with the oil in a large bowl. Add the chicken and onion and turn until they are coated all over. Leave to marinate while you cook the couscous.

Remove the grill plate from the air fryer's basket. Add the couscous, butter and warm water to the basket. Give the handle a shake so all the couscous is covered in the water and evenly distributed in the basket. Cook at 200°C (400°F) for 5 minutes, stirring halfway through cooking. Remove and divide between two serving plates and cover loosely with a piece of foil. Set aside.

Add the marinated chicken and onion to the basket (there's no need to clean the basket) and cook at 190°C (375°F) for 10 minutes, stirring halfway through cooking.

Add the garlic, chopped tomatoes, tomato purée, warm water, stock cube and apricots. Stir everything together, then cook for a further 10 minutes, stirring halfway through cooking, and check if the chicken is cooked through.

Serve the chicken tagine on top of the couscous with a sprinkling of pistachios.

photograph on previous page

FOR THE COUSCOUS
175 g (6 oz/scant 1 cup) couscous
knob of butter
225 ml (7½ fl oz/scant 1 cup)
  warm water

FOR THE TAGINE
2 teaspoons ras-el-hanout
  spice mix
1 tablespoon cooking oil
2 boneless chicken thighs, skin on
1 red onion, halved and sliced
1 garlic clove, crushed
2 tomatoes, chopped
1 tablespoon tomato purée
  (paste)
200 ml (7 fl oz/scant 1 cup) warm
  water
½ chicken stock cube
6 dried apricots, halved
2 tablespoons shelled unsalted
  pistachio nuts, roughly chopped

If you have a dual basket air fryer then you can cook the couscous at the same time as the chicken. If not, then cook the couscous first and set aside.

Chicken Schnitzel

/ Serves 2 / Ready in 30 minutes /

Slice each chicken breast lengthways so it opens out like a book and continue to slice all the way through into two pieces. Put the chicken pieces between two sheets of cling film (plastic wrap) and, using a rolling pin, bash each piece until it is 5 mm (¼ in) thick.

Spread the flour out on a large plate and sprinkle over 1 large pinch of salt and a few grinds of black pepper. Pour the beaten eggs into a shallow bowl. Spread the breadcrumbs out on a third plate and mix with another large pinch of salt.

Dip each piece of chicken into the seasoned flour, turning it over to fully coat, then dip into the egg, turning over a few times to drench them. Finally, dip into the breadcrumbs, turning over a few times until the pieces are completely coated.

Depending on the size of your air fryer you may need to cook the schnitzels in batches. Add the schnitzels to the air fryer's grill plate in a singer layer. Spray generously with oil and cook at 200°C (400°F) for 5 minutes. Turn the schnitzels over, spray again with oil and cook for a further 5 minutes, or until cooked through.

Serve with a sprinkling of parsley and a side of lemon wedges for squeezing over.

2 skinless, boneless chicken breasts
60 g (2 oz/½ cup) plain (all-purpose) flour
2 large pinches of salt
freshly ground black pepper
2 eggs, beaten
100 g (3½ oz/1 cup) dried breadcrumbs (I used Paxo Golden Breadcrumbs)
cooking oil spray

TO SERVE
small handful of fresh parsley, chopped
1 lemon, cut into wedges

Ricotta and Herb Stuffed Chicken Breast with Rosemary Potatoes

/ Serves 2 / Ready in 30 minutes /

Mix the ricotta, herbs, garlic and salt together in a large bowl.

Cut a deep incision, about 5 cm (2 in) in length along the side of each chicken breast. Divide the ricotta mixture evenly between the breasts, stuffing it into the pockets.

Spray each piece of chicken with oil. Lay 3 rashers of bacon flat on a chopping board, slightly overlapping. Put one chicken breast into the centre, upside-down, and fold the bacon around so you have a wrapped breast. Repeat with the second chicken breast.

Carefully lay the stuffed chicken breasts onto the grill plate, seam-side down, and cook at 180°C (350°F) for 10 minutes. Turn the breasts over, seam-side up, and cook for a further 8 minutes. The chicken is done when it's cooked through and the bacon is golden. Leave to rest, loosely covered in foil while you cook the potatoes.

In a bowl, mix the potatoes with the rosemary, salt and oil. Transfer the coated potatoes to the air fryer basket and cook at 200°C (400°F) for 15 minutes, shaking the basket a couple of times during cooking.

Serve the stuffed chicken with the rosemary potatoes.

4 tablespoons ricotta
1 teaspoon dried mixed herbs
1 garlic clove, crushed
pinch of salt
2 skinless, boneless chicken breasts
cooking oil spray
6 rashers of streaky bacon

FOR THE POTATOES
2 roasting potatoes, peeled and cut into bite-size pieces
1 rosemary stalk, needles finely chopped
2 pinches of salt
2 teaspoons cooking oil

If you have a dual basket air fryer, then cook the potatoes at the same time as the chicken. If not, then cook the potatoes while the chicken rests.

Chicken Pot Pie

You will need
a round pie tin (pan)
that fits inside your
air fryer's basket.
I used a 20 cm (8 in)
ceramic pie dish.

/ Serves 2 / Ready in 45 minutes /

Remove the grill plate from the air fryer's basket. Add the oil, chicken, carrot, onion, celery, thyme, garlic, salt and a good grinding of pepper to the basket. Stir everything together and cook at 180°C (350°F) for 15 minutes, stirring a couple of times during cooking.

Stir in the crème fraîche, Marmite, peas, parsley and warm water and cook for a further for 4 minutes.

Spoon the filling into the pie dish. Leave to cool, using the refrigerator to speed up the process. Meanwhile, clean the air fryer's basket.

Once the filling is cooled to room temperature, roll out the pastry. Gently lift and cover the pie. Use your fingers or a fork to crimp the edges around the dish to seal the pastry lid. Brush the pastry with the beaten egg to glaze. Using the tip of a sharp knife, make three small slits in the pastry to let out steam while cooking.

Carefully lift the pie into the air fryer's basket and cook at 180°C (350°F) for 20 minutes, or until the pie is golden and the filling is piping hot. Leave to stand for a few minutes, then dig in!

2 tablespoons cooking oil
2 skinless, boneless chicken
 breasts, cut into bite-size pieces
1 carrot, thinly sliced
1 onion, finely chopped
1 celery stalk, thinly sliced
½ teaspoon thyme leaves or
 dried thyme
1 garlic clove, crushed
large pinch of salt
freshly ground black pepper
5 tablespoons crème fraîche
1 teaspoon Marmite or yeast
 extract
50 g (1¾ oz/⅓ cup) frozen peas
1 tablespoon chopped fresh
 parsley
1 tablespoon warm water
320 g (11 oz) ready-rolled
 shortcrust pastry
1 egg, beaten

Roast Dinner

If you have a dual basket air fryer, then cook the potatoes and vegetables at the same time as the chicken. Otherwise, cook them when the chicken is finished cooking.

/ Serves 2 / Ready in 50 minutes /

Rub the chicken all over with the oil, then season with the salt and a few grinds of pepper. Sprinkle over the dried herbs, adding some to the cavity of the chicken as well. Put the chicken breast side down onto the air fryer's grill plate and cook at 190°C (375°F) for 20 minutes. Carefully turn the chicken over, using tongs and a fork, and cook at 200°C (400°F) for a further 20 minutes, or until the chicken is cooked through (if you have a meat thermometer it should read at least 74°C/165°F).

Meanwhile, drain the potatoes. In a large bowl, mix them with the carrot, oil and salt. If you have a free basket, then start cooking the vegetables. Remove the air fryer's grill plate. Add the potatoes and carrot and cook at 200°C (400°F) for 10 minutes, shaking halfway through cooking.

Stir the onion into the potatoes and carrot and cook again at 200°C (400°F) for 5 minutes. Finally, add the green beans, stir everything together and cook at 200°C (400°F) for 8 minutes, stirring halfway through cooking.

Once the chicken is cooked, carefully lift it out of the air fryer onto a serving dish or chopping board and leave to rest. Remove the grill plate; be careful, it's very hot! Tip out the excess fat, then pour the ready-made gravy into the basket. Lift the chicken again and, using tongs and a fork, tilt it to drain the juices from the cavity into the gravy. Stir the gravy and cooking juices together and cook at 180°C (350°F) for 3 minutes. Pour into a serving jug.

Add the Yorkshire puddings to the air fryer's basket and cook at 200°C (400°F) for 2–5 minutes, depending on the packet's instructions.

Serve the roast chicken with the vegetables, gravy and Yorkshire puddings.

FOR THE CHICKEN
1.4 kg (3 lb) whole small chicken
2 teaspoons cooking oil
large pinch of salt
freshly ground black pepper
1 teaspoon dried mixed herbs

FOR THE VEGETABLES
2 roasting potatoes, peeled and quartered and soaked in warm water until ready to use
1 large carrot, roughly chopped
1 tablespoon cooking oil
large pinch of salt
1 small red onion, cut into 6 wedges
75 g (2½ oz) green beans

FOR THE GRAVY AND YORKSHIRE PUDDINGS
½ x 350 g (12 oz) pouch ready-made chicken gravy
2–4 ready-made Yorkshire puddings

DIY TAKEAWAY

Chicken Chow Mein

/ Serves 2 / Ready in 20 minutes /

In a bowl, mix the oil with the chicken and 1 tablespoon of the soy sauce.

Remove the air fryer's grill plate. Add the marinated chicken to the basket in a single layer and cook at 200°C (400°F) for 5 minutes, stirring halfway through.

Add the vegetables to the chicken and spread the mixture out evenly. Cook for 6 minutes, stirring halfway through cooking.

Add the remaining soy sauce, the honey, ginger, garlic, sesame oil and noodles to the basket. Depending on what type of noodles you are using you may have difficulty stirring them in. To help with this, cook for 1 minute to soften the noodles, then stir everything together really well so that the noodles are separated and everything is covered in the sauce. Cook for a further 2 minutes and serve.

1 tablespoon cooking oil
1 skinless, boneless chicken breast, thinly sliced
2 tablespoons dark soy sauce
1 carrot, thinly sliced
3 spring onions (scallions), cut into 5 cm (2 in) pieces
6 baby corn, halved lengthways if large
1 red (bell) pepper, thinly sliced
1 teaspoon runny honey
1 teaspoon ginger purée
1 garlic clove, finely chopped
2 teaspoons toasted sesame oil
300 g (10½ oz) packet straight to wok/quick-cook medium noodles

Fried Chicken and Chips

If you have a dual basket air fryer, then cook the chips at the same time as the chicken. If not, then |cook the chips after the chicken while it rests.

/ Serves 2 / Ready in 45 minutes, plus marinating /

Add the chicken and buttermilk to a large bowl or a large plastic bag, cover or seal and marinate in the refrigerator for at least 1 hour, or up to 24 hours.

When ready to cook the chicken, make the seasoned flour. Mix the plain flour, cornflour, paprika, garlic powder, ginger, mustard powder, celery salt, mixed herbs, salt and white pepper together in a large bowl.

Have a plate or chopping board ready to put your battered chicken on. Remove the chicken from the buttermilk, then coat all over in the seasoned flour by turning each piece over in it a few times. Set aside on a plate.

To cook the chips, add the chips to a large heatproof bowl and pour in enough hot water to cover them completely. Leave for 10 minutes, then drain and pat dry with paper towels. Transfer them to a large bowl, add the oil and salt and stir so every chip is evenly covered.

Spray the air fryer's grill plate with cooking oil. Add the chicken pieces in a singer layer and spray each piece generously with oil. Cook at 200°C (400°F) for 20 minutes, carefully turning the pieces over after 10 minutes and continue to cook for another 10 minutes or until the chicken is cooked through. I find using two forks the easiest way to do this and doesn't break the batter.

Cook the chips for 18 minutes at 190°C (375°F), shaking the basket halfway through cooking. The chicken and chips should be finished cooking at roughly the same time if you are using a dual basket air fryer. Serve with your favourite condiments.

FOR THE CHICKEN
2 chicken drumsticks, skin on
2 chicken thighs, skin on
150 ml (5 fl oz/scant ⅔ cup) buttermilk (if you can't find buttermilk then mix 125 ml (4 fl oz/½ cup) whole milk with 1 tablespoon lemon juice or white wine vinegar)
125 g (4½ oz/1 cup) plain (all-purpose) flour
2 tablespoons cornflour (cornstarch)
1 tablespoon paprika
2 teaspoons garlic powder or granules
1 teaspoon ground ginger
1 teaspoon dry English mustard powder
1 teaspoon celery salt
1 teaspoon dried mixed herbs
1 teaspoon salt
1 teaspoon ground white pepper
cooking oil spray
condiments of choice, to serve

FOR THE CHIPS
2 roasting potatoes, peeled and cut into roughly 1 cm (½ in) thick chips
1 tablespoon cooking oil
large pinch of salt

Tikka Tandoori Kebabs with Raita

/ Makes 4 kebabs / Ready in 20 minutes

Mix the yoghurt, tandoori masala, ketchup and salt together in a large bowl. Add the chicken and stir to coat all over.

Thread the chicken onto four skewers. Lay the skewers on the air fryer's grill plate or if you have an air fryer rack for skewers then use that. Spray with oil and cook at 200°C (400°F) for 12 minutes, turning halfway through cooking.

Meanwhile, make the raita. In a bowl, mix the yoghurt with the mint, cucumber, red onion and salt.

Serve the skewers alongside the raita and enjoy.

4 tablespoons plain yoghurt
1 tablespoon tandoori masala powder
1 tablespoon tomato ketchup
large pinch of salt
2 skinless, boneless chicken breasts or 4 skinless, boneless chicken thighs, thinly sliced
cooking oil spray

FOR THE RAITA
150 ml (5 fl oz) plain yoghurt
handful of mint leaves, chopped
¼ cucumber, halved lengthways, seeded and finely chopped
¼ red onion, finely chopped
pinch of salt

You can use metal or wooden skewers but they must fit inside your air fryer's basket. If using wooden skewers, then break them to the size needed and soak them in a bowl of cold water for at least 5 minutes.

Bang Bang Chicken

/ Serves 2 / Ready in 30 minutes /

Mix the paprika, dried mixed herbs, garlic powder and salt together in a large bowl. Add the chicken and turn until it is coated all over.

For the crunch, crush the cornflakes by pounding them in a large bowl using the end of a rolling pin. Mix the crushed cornflakes with the paprika, mixed herbs and garlic powder.

Add the beaten eggs to a wide shallow dish.

Have a plate ready to put your coated chicken pieces on. Start by dipping the chicken into the eggs. Turn the pieces over a couple of times to make sure every side is covered in egg, then add the chicken to the seasoned cornflakes, again turning them over and making sure every side is coated. For extra crunch, dip the pieces back into the egg and then again into the cornflakes. Set aside on the plate.

Remove the air fryer's grill plate and spray the basket with oil. Add the chicken pieces in a single layer and spray the chicken all over with oil. Cook at 200°C (400°F) for 12 minutes, carefully turning the pieces over halfway through cooking.

Meanwhile, to make the sauce, mix all the ingredients together in a large bowl.

When the chicken has finished cooking add it to the bowl with the sauce and gently toss until it is coated all over. Serve with a sprinkling of chopped chives.

1 teaspoon paprika
1 teaspoon dried mixed herbs
  or dried oregano
1 teaspoon garlic powder
  or granules
1 teaspoon salt
2 skinless, boneless chicken
  breasts, cut into large
  bite-size pieces
cooking oil spray
small handful of chives, chopped,
  to serve

FOR THE CRUNCH
100 g (3½ oz/3⅓ cups) cornflakes
1 teaspoon paprika
1 teaspoon mixed herbs
  or oregano
1 teaspoon garlic powder
  or granules
2 eggs, beaten

FOR THE BANG BANG SAUCE
120 ml (4 fl oz/½ cup) mayonnaise
4 tablespoons sweet chilli sauce
1 tablespoon runny honey
2 tablespoons sriracha sauce
1 tablespoon rice wine vinegar
  or white wine vinegar

Chicken Bean Burritos

/ Makes 4 / Ready in 30 minutes /

Mix the oil, garlic powder, ¼ teaspoon salt, smoked paprika and ground cumin together in a large bowl. Add the chicken breasts and stir to coat all over.

In another bowl, mix the black beans with the cayenne pepper, sweetcorn, spring onions and coriander. Add the rice straight from the pouch and stir until the mixture is well combined and all the clumps of rice have broken up.

In a third bowl, mash the avocado, then stir through the lime juice and a large pinch of salt. Set aside.

Add the marinated chicken to the air fryer's grill plate in a single layer and cook at 200°C (400°F) for 18 minutes.

Slice through the thickest part of the chicken to check the fibres are set and the chicken is cooked. Once cooked, thinly slice the chicken, then pour over any cooking juices left in the air fryer.

Lay out the wraps on a work surface. Evenly distribute the bean and rice mixture down the centre of each wrap, leaving a border. Repeat with the chicken, then the grated cheese and finish with the guacamole and a few shakes of hot sauce. Brush around the edges of each tortilla with beaten egg. Working with one wrap at a time, fold the ends in, then fold one of the free ends over the filling and continue rolling tightly until the burrito is fully wrapped. Repeat with the remaining wraps.

Using both hands, transfer the burritos to the air fryer and cook at 200°C (400°F) for 3 minutes. You may need to do this in batches depending on the size of your air fryer.

Serve warm with extra hot sauce.

photograph on previous page

1 tablespoon cooking oil
¼ teaspoon garlic powder or granules
salt
½ teaspoon smoked paprika
½ teaspoon ground cumin
2 skinless, boneless chicken breasts, cut in half lengthways
200 g (7 oz) tinned black beans, drained and rinsed
½ teaspoon cayenne pepper
2 heaped tablespoons tinned sweetcorn
2 spring onions (scallions), chopped
handful of coriander (cilantro), chopped
250 g (9 oz) pouch microwave basmati rice (I used Tilda Pure Basmati Rice)
1 avocado
juice of 1 lime
4 large tortilla wraps
6 tablespoons grated Cheddar
12 shakes of hot sauce, plus extra to serve (I used Cholula Original)
1 egg, beaten

Red Thai Chicken Curry

If you have a dual basket air fryer, then cook the rice at the same time as the chicken curry.

/ Serves 2 / Ready in 40 minutes /

Mix the curry paste, coconut cream, salt, sugar and a few grinds of black pepper together in a large bowl. Stir in the chicken, carrot and red onion. Cover and leave to marinate while you cook the rice.

Remove the air fryer's grill plate from the basket. Add the rice and water to the basket and stir together. Cook at 200°C (400°F) for 2 minutes, or until piping hot. Divide equally between two serving bowls and set aside.

Add the chicken curry mixture to the basket (there's no need to wash it), spreading it out in an even layer and cook at 200°C (400°F) for 10 minutes.

Turn the chicken pieces over and any vegetables that are starting to char too much. Add the water around the chicken and vegetables and cook again at 200°C (400°F) for a further 8 minutes, or until the chicken is cooked through.

When the cooking time is finished, stir the curry with a wooden spoon, then divide between the two bowls of rice, sprinkle with the coriander and serve.

FOR THE CURRY
4 tablespoons Thai red curry paste
160 ml (5½ fl oz) coconut cream
½ teaspoon salt
¼ teaspoon caster (superfine) sugar
freshly ground black pepper
2 skinless, boneless chicken breasts, sliced
1 carrot, sliced
1 small red onion, halved and sliced
2 tablespoons water
small handful of coriander (cilantro), roughly chopped, to serve

FOR THE RICE
250 g (9 oz) pouch microwave jasmine rice (I used Tilda Fragrant Jasmine Rice)
2 tablespoons water

Caribbean Chicken with Plantain

If your have a dual basket air fryer, then cook the plantain at the same time as the chicken. If you do not, then cook the plantain after the chicken while the chicken rests.

/ Serves 2 / Ready in 30 minutes /

Mix the garlic, onion, salt, allspice, nutmeg, thyme, chilli, soy sauce and brown sugar together in a large bowl. Add the chicken and stir to coat each piece all over.

Line the air fryer's grill plate with baking parchment. Lay the chicken on the grill plate in one layer and cook at 180°C (350°F) for 20 minutes, turning the chicken over halfway through cooking.

Turn the chicken over again and drizzle the honey over the pieces. Cook for a further 5 minutes or until the chicken is cooked through when checked.

If using the same air fryer for the plantain, then remove the chicken's baking parchment and line the air fryer with a new sheet of baking parchment. Arrange the plantain in a single layer and spray generously with oil. Cook at 200°C (400°F) for 6 minutes. Using two forks, turn the slices over, spray again with oil and cook for a further 6 minutes, or until golden and soft.

Pour any cooking juices left in the air fryer over the top of the chicken and serve with the plantain and lime wedges.

2 garlic cloves, crushed
1 onion, grated
1 teaspoon salt
½ teaspoon allspice
good grating of nutmeg
1 teaspoon dried thyme
½ Scotch bonnet or 1 red chilli, finely chopped
1 tablespoon dark soy sauce
1 tablespoon soft brown sugar
2 chicken drumsticks, skin on
2 boneless chicken thighs, skin on
1 tablespoon runny honey
1 blackening ripe plantain, cut into 5 mm (¼ in) slices
cooking oil spray
lime wedges, to serve

Bacon Chicken Burger with Grilled Onions

/ Serves 2 / Ready in 20 minutes /

Remove the air fryer's grill plate and add the onion and cooking oil to the basket. Mix together, then cook at 180°C (350°F) for 8 minutes, stirring halfway through. Stir in the sugar and salt and increase the temperature to 200°C (400°F) and cook for a further 2 minutes, or until golden. Remove and set aside.

Give the air fryer's basket a quick wipe, then add the grill plate back in. Arrange the bacon rashers flat on the grill plate in a single layer and not touching each other. Cook at 180°C (350°F) for 5 minutes. Remove, cut each rasher in half and set aside.

Mix the chicken mince, onion granules, Worcestershire sauce and salt together in a large bowl. Divide the mixture into two equal portions, then shape into burger patties slightly wider than the buns. Press your thumb in the middle of each patty to make an indentation. This will help the patty keep its shape when cooking.

Add the patties to the grill plate. There's no need to wash off the bacon grease. Spray with oil and cook at 200°C (400°F) for 5 minutes. Flip the patties over and cook for a further 3 minutes, or until cooked through.

Divide the grated cheese between the burgers and close the air fryer for 2 minutes. The heat inside the air fryer will melt the cheese. Remove and set aside.

Spread the bottom buns with mayonnaise and cook at 200°C (400°F) for 1 minute. Remove, add the top buns and close the air fryer for 1 minute.

Assemble the burgers: bottom bun, patty with cheese, onion, bacon and top buns. Serve with your favourite condiments.

FOR THE ONIONS
1 onion, thinly sliced
2 teaspoons cooking oil
1 teaspoon caster (superfine) sugar
pinch of salt

FOR THE BURGERS
3 rashers of streaky bacon
250 g (9 oz) minced (ground) chicken or turkey
1 teaspoon onion granules
1 teaspoon Worcestershire sauce
½ teaspoon salt
cooking oil spray
4 heaped tablespoons grated Cheddar
2 burger buns, sliced
2 tablespoons mayonnaise
condiments of choice, to serve

If you have a dual basket air fryer, then cook the onions at the same time as the burgers.

Lemon Chicken with Rice

If you have a dual basket air fryer, you can cook the rice at the same time as the chicken.

/ Serves 2 as a main or 4 as a side dish / Ready in 30 minutes /

In a large bowl, mix the chicken with the soy sauce and sesame oil.

Mix the flour, lemon zest and a few grinds of black pepper together in another large bowl. Beat the egg in a wide shallow bowl or plate. Finally, spread the panko breadcrumbs out on a plate.

Remove the chicken from the marinade and add it to the seasoned flour. Coat the chicken all over in the flour, then dip the chicken into the egg, again coating it all over. Finally, add the chicken to the breadcrumbs, turning the pieces over a few times to coat.

Remove the grill plate from the air fryer's basket and spray the basket with oil. Add the chicken pieces to the basket and spray all over with oil. Cook at 200°C (400°F) for 10 minutes, turning the chicken over halfway through cooking.

Meanwhile, to make the sauce, mix the melted butter, honey, soy sauce, cornflour and the juice from the zested lemon together in a large bowl. Stir in the hot water.

Remove the chicken from the basket. Pour in the sauce and cook at 200°C (400°F) for 5 minutes, stirring halfway through cooking.

The sauce will still be runny but add the chicken back to the basket and stir into the sauce. Cook again at 200°C (400°F) for 4 minutes.

Divide the saucy chicken among serving plates or a platter and cook the rice. There's no need to clean the basket. Add the rice to the air fryer and stir in the water. Cook at 200°C (400°F) for 2–4 minutes until cooked to your liking.

Serve the chicken with a sprinkling of spring onions alongside the rice.

4 skinless, boneless chicken thighs, cut into bite-size pieces
2 teaspoons dark soy sauce
2 teaspoons toasted sesame oil
2 tablespoons plain (all-purpose) flour
zest and juice of 1 lemon
freshly ground black pepper
1 egg
70 g (2½ oz/generous 1 cup) panko breadcrumbs
cooking oil spray

FOR THE SAUCE
25 g (1 oz) butter, melted
1 tablespoon runny honey
2 teaspoons dark soy sauce
1 tablespoon cornflour (cornstarch)
100 ml (3½ fl oz/scant ½ cup) hot water

TO SERVE
250 g (9 oz) pouch microwave basmati rice (I used Tilda Pure Basmati Rice)
2 tablespoons water
2 spring onions (scallions), sliced

Chicken Nuggets

/ Makes about 20 / Ready in 20 minutes /

Mix the cornflour, salt and a few grinds of black pepper together in a large bowl. Add the chicken and coat each piece all over in the seasoned flour.

Beat the egg in a wide shallow bowl. In another large bowl, mix the breadcrumbs with the smoked paprika and garlic powder.

Have a large plate or chopping board ready to put your finished nuggets on. First dip each piece of chicken in the egg, coating it all over, then in the breadcrumbs, making sure each piece is evenly coated.

Spray the air fryer's grill plate with oil. Lay the nuggets out in a single layer and spray them generously with oil. Cook at 200°C (400°F) for 10 minutes, turning the pieces over halfway through the cooking and spraying again with the oil.

Serve with your favourite dipping sauce.

2 tablespoons cornflour (cornstarch)
large pinch of salt
freshly ground black pepper
2 skinless, boneless chicken breasts, cut into large bite-size pieces
1 egg
100 g (3½ oz/1 cup) shop-bought golden breadcrumbs (I used Paxo)
½ teaspoon smoked paprika
½ teaspoon garlic powder or granules
cooking oil spray
dipping sauce, such as tomato ketchup or mayonnaise, to serve

Shawarma Wrap

/ Serves 4 / Ready in 30 minutes /

Mix the oil, garlic, lemon juice, spices and salt together in a large bowl. Add the chicken and coat all over. Cover and leave to marinate while you make the sauce.

In a bowl, mix the mayonnaise with the yoghurt, lemon juice, garlic and mint. Set aside.

Lay the marinated chicken in a single layer on the air fryer's grill plate in the basket. Cook at 200°C (400°F) for 20 minutes, turning the chicken over after 10 minutes and then continue cooking for another 10 minutes or until the chicken is cooked through (check to see if the fibres are set by making a small cut into the thickest part of the chicken).

Remove the chicken and thinly slice before putting on a plate. Pour the leftover cooking juices from the air fryer's basket over the chicken.

Lay out the flatbreads on a work surface, spoon over the sauce then divide the chicken between each one, adding pickles and salad. Fold the bread over the mixture and fold in each end. Tightly roll up into a wrap, slice in half and serve.

2 tablespoons cooking oil
3 garlic cloves, crushed
juice of 1 lemon
2 teaspoons paprika
2 teaspoons ground cumin
1 teaspoon ground coriander
1 teaspoon sumac
¼ teaspoon chilli (hot pepper) flakes
1 teaspoon salt
700 g (1 lb 9 oz) skinless, boneless chicken thighs

FOR THE SAUCE
3 tablespoons mayonnaise
110 g (3½ oz) Greek-style plain yoghurt
juice of ½ lemon
1 garlic clove, crushed
handful of mint leaves, finely chopped

TO SERVE
4 large flatbreads or pitta breads
your choice of pickles (I like pickled red onion, cabbage and green chillies)
your choice of salad (I like mixed leaves and sliced tomatoes)

TO SHARE

Honey Garlic Drumsticks

/ Makes about 12 pieces / Ready in 30 minutes /

Add the drumsticks to a large bowl and sprinkle over the cornflour, garlic and salt. Toss everything together to coat well.

You may need to work in batches. Remove the grill plate, then arrange the drumsticks in the air fryer's basket in a single layer. Spray all over with oil and cook at 190°C (375°F) for 15 minutes, turning over and spraying again halfway through cooking.

Meanwhile, discard any leftover cornflour mixture (there's no need to wash the bowl), then add the ginger, soy sauce, honey and sesame oil to the bowl and mix together.

Carefully pour the sauce over the partially cooked chicken and turn each drumstick over a few times so that each is coated all over. Cook again at 190°C (375°F) for 10 minutes, turning the chicken over halfway through cooking. Test the chicken is cooked through – make a small cut and check to see if the fibres are set.

Transfer the cooked drumsticks to a serving platter and spoon over the sauce left in the basket. Sprinkle over the sesame seeds and serve.

1 kg (2 lb 4 oz) chicken drumsticks, skin on
2 tablespoons cornflour (cornstarch)
1 teaspoon garlic powder or granules
pinch of salt
cooking oil spray
1 tablespoon grated fresh ginger
3 tablespoons light soy sauce
3 tablespoons runny honey
1 teaspoon sesame oil
1 teaspoon toasted sesame seeds

Chicken Satay with Peanut Dipping Sauce

/ Makes 4 skewers / Ready in 20 minutes /

Mix the chicken, curry powder, coconut milk, soy sauce and sugar together in a large bowl.

Thread the chicken evenly between four metal or wooden skewers.

Spray the air fryer's grill plate with oil. Add the skewers or if you have an air fryer rack for skewers, then use that. Cook at 200°C (400°F) for 12 minutes, turning halfway through cooking.

Meanwhile, make the dipping sauce. In a bowl, mix the peanut butter with the soy sauce, chilli sauce, sugar and lime juice until a thick paste. Stir in 1–2 tablespoons of hot water to loosen it.

Serve the satay skewers with the lime wedges and either the sauce on the side or drizzled on top.

2 skinless, boneless chicken breasts or 4 skinless, boneless chicken thighs, sliced
1 tablespoon mild curry powder
2 tablespoons coconut milk
1 tablespoon soy sauce
1 teaspoon caster (superfine) sugar
cooking oil spray

FOR THE DIPPING SAUCE
3 tablespoons peanut butter (crunchy or smooth, whatever your preference is)
1 tablespoon dark soy sauce
1 tablespoon sweet chilli sauce
1 lime, ½ juiced and ½ cut into wedges
1–2 tablespoons hot water

You can use metal or wooden skewers but they must fit inside your air fryer's basket. If using wooden skewers, then break them to the size needed and soak in a bowl of cold water for at least 5 minutes.

Chinese Chicken Sausage Rolls

/ **Makes about 18 rolls** / **Ready in 30 minutes** /

Mix the mince, soy sauce, honey, sesame oil, spring onions, Chinese 5 spice and salt together in a large bowl.

Gently roll out the pastry, leaving it on the baking parchment. Cut it in half lengthways.

Spread the meat mixture down each length. Brush the edges with the beaten egg, then fold over one side of the pastry and seal using a fork if there is excess pastry. If not, then make sure the pastry edges are overlapping each other. Sprinkle over the sesame seeds and cut into 4 cm (1½ in) long rolls. There will be about 18 rolls in total.

Cook in batches using the air fryer's rack if you have one. If not, then arrange the air fryer's grill plate and cook at 190°C (375°F) for 10 minutes, or until dark golden and cooked through.

Serve warm with your choice of dipping sauce.

400 g (14 oz) minced (ground) chicken (turkey mince works too)
3 tablespoons dark soy sauce
1 teaspoon runny honey
1 teaspoon sesame oil
3 spring onions (scallions), thinly sliced
½ teaspoon Chinese 5 spice
pinch of salt
320 g (11 oz) ready-rolled puff pastry (I used Jus Rol)
1 egg, beaten
1 tablespoon black sesame seeds
soy sauce or sriracha sauce, to serve

Pesto Chicken Crostini

/ **Makes about 16 slices** / **Ready in 30 minutes** /

Toast the baguette slices on the grill plate in the air fryer at 200°C (400°F) for 2 minutes. Turn the pieces over and toast for a further 2 minutes. Remove and set aside.

For the pesto, in a pestle and mortar (or bowl and the end of a rolling pin), pound the garlic with a large pinch of salt. Add the chopped basil and grind to a paste. Add the pine nuts, Parmesan and 1 tablespoon of the oil, then pound and grind again. Stir in the remaining tablespoon of oil, then taste and season with salt and pepper, if needed.

In a bowl, coat the chicken strips with about half of the pesto (about 1 heaped tablespoon).

Line the air fryer's grill plate with baking parchment. Arrange the chicken in a singer layer on the parchment and cook at 200°C (400°F) for 10 minutes, turning over halfway through cooking.

Meanwhile, stir the mayonnaise into the leftover pesto.

Once the chicken is finished cooking, leave the pieces in the basket, then brush them with half of the pesto mayonnaise. Close the air fryer and let the chicken rest for 5 minutes.

Meanwhile, add about ½ teaspoon of the remaining pesto mayonnaise to each crostini.

Once rested, thinly slice the chicken, then divide between the crostini. Top each with a quarter of a cherry tomato, then sprinkle with basil leaves and serve.

photograph on previous page

1 small baguette/baguettine, cut into 1 cm (½ in) thick slices
1 skinless, boneless chicken breast, sliced lengthways into 3 strips
3 tablespoons mayonnaise
4 cherry tomatoes, quartered
handful of small basil leaves

FOR THE PESTO
1 small garlic clove, roughly chopped
salt and freshly ground black pepper
large handful of basil, roughly chopped
1 tablespoon toasted pine nuts
2 heaped tablespoons grated Parmesan
2 tablespoons extra virgin olive oil

Popcorn Chicken

/ Serves 2 as a main or 4 for sharing / Ready in 45 minutes, plus marinating /

Mix the garlic powder, salt and buttermilk together in a large bowl until evenly combined. Add the chicken pieces, cover and marinate in the refrigerator for at least 1 hour and up to 24 hours.

Once you're ready to cook, in large shallow bowl, mix the flour with the cornflour, paprika, onion granules, salt and white pepper.

Have a large plate or chopping board ready to put your finished pieces of chicken on. Add the egg to the chicken mixture and stir, then remove the chicken from the buttermilk mixture and add it to the seasoned flour, turning until it is coated all over. Add the chicken back to the buttermilk mixture, then for a second time, add the chicken to the flour and turn to coat.

Add the chicken in a single layer to the air fryer's grill plate. Spray generously with oil so every piece is covered and cook at 200°C (400°F) for 12 minutes, turning the pieces over halfway through cooking and spraying again with oil.

Serve with your favourite dipping sauce.

1 teaspoon garlic powder or granules
½ teaspoon salt
100 ml (3½ fl oz/scant ½ cup) buttermilk (if you can't find buttermilk then mix 100 ml (3½ fl oz/scant ½ cup) whole milk with 1 tablespoon lemon juice or white wine vinegar)
2 skinless, boneless chicken breasts, cut into bite-size pieces
125 g (4½ oz/1 cup) plain (all-purpose) flour
2 tablespoons cornflour (cornstarch)
½ teaspoon paprika
2 teaspoons onion granules
1 teaspoon salt
½ teaspoon ground white pepper
1 egg, beaten
cooking oil spray
dipping sauces of choice, to serve

Mediterranean Chicken Skewers

/ Makes 4 skewers / Ready in 20 minutes /

Mix the chicken, olive oil, lemon juice, garlic, oregano, rosemary, red onion and red pepper together in a large bowl. Add a pinch of salt and a few grinds of pepper and stir again.

Thread the chicken and vegetables onto four metal or wooden skewers. Lay the skewers on the air fryer's grill plate or if you have an air fryer rack for skewers, then use that. Cook at 200°C (400°F) for 12 minutes, turning halfway through cooking.

Meanwhile, to make the dip, in a bowl, mix the yoghurt with the mint and salt and a few grinds of pepper. Set aside until ready to serve.

Serve the skewers with the mint yoghurt dip and enjoy!

2 skinless, boneless chicken breasts, cut into bite-size pieces
2 tablespoons olive oil
2 tablespoons lemon juice
1 garlic clove, crushed
½ teaspoon dried oregano
1 rosemary stalk, leaves finely chopped
½ red onion, cut into bite-size pieces
½ red (bell) pepper, cut into bite-size pieces
salt and freshly ground black pepper

FOR THE MINT YOGHURT DIP
4 heaped tablespoons Greek yoghurt
handful of mint leaves, chopped
large pinch of salt

You can use metal or wooden skewers but they must fit inside your air fryer's basket. If using wooden, then break them to the size needed and soak in a bowl of cold water for at least 5 minutes.

Chicken Fried Rice

Mix the cooking oil, chicken, onion, Chinese 5 spice and soy sauces together in a large bowl.

Remove the air fryer's grill plate, add the mixture to the basket and spread out into an even layer. Cook at 180°C (350°F) for 10 minutes, stirring halfway through cooking.

Add the rice, garlic, frozen vegetables and sesame oil to the chicken mixture. Stir well so everything is coated in the soy dressing and the rice is broken up. Cook at 180°C (350°F) for 6 minutes, stirring halfway through.

Serve with a sprinkling of spring onions and enjoy!

1 tablespoon cooking oil
1 skinless, boneless chicken breast, sliced
1 small onion, halved and finely sliced
1 teaspoon Chinese 5 spice
1 tablespoon dark soy sauce
1 tablespoon light soy sauce
250 g (9 oz) pouch microwave long-grain rice, squeeze pouch to break up the rice
1 garlic clove, finely chopped
100 g (3½ oz) frozen mixed vegetables
1 teaspoon sesame oil
2 spring onions (scallions), sliced, to serve

Chicken and Chorizo Empanadas

/ Makes 6 empanadas / Ready in 30 minutes /

Mix the chicken, spring onions, tomato, garlic, cumin, chorizo, olives, oil and salt together in a large bowl.

Remove the grill plate from the air fryer. Add the chicken mixture to the basket and spread it out in an even layer. Cook at 200°C (400°F) for 10 minutes, stirring halfway through cooking.

Remove the chicken mixture from the basket and leave to cool in a bowl, refrigerating it to speed up the process.

Roll out the pastry. Using a 12 cm (4½ in) cookie cutter or template, cut out six rounds from the sheet of pastry. You may need to cut out the first four and then re-roll the leftover pastry to get the last two rounds.

Add a heaped tablespoon of the chicken mixture to each round, or until it is all used up. Fold the pastry over the filling to make a half-moon, then using a fork, crimp the rounded edge of the pastry to seal together. Repeat with the remaining empanadas. Brush all over with beaten egg.

Cook in batches if needed. Replace the grill plate in the air fryer's basket and arrange the empanadas on the grill without touching each other. Cook at 200°C (400°F) for 8 minutes, or until dark golden in colour. If the underside looks underdone, turn the empanadas over and cook for a further 1–2 minutes. Enjoy!

1 skinless, boneless chicken breast, cut into small bite-size pieces
2 spring onions (scallions), sliced
1 tomato, chopped
1 garlic clove, crushed
¼ teaspoon ground cumin
50 g (1¾ oz) dry-cured chorizo sausage, cut into small bite-size pieces
6 pitted green olives, chopped
1 teaspoon cooking oil
pinch of salt
320 g (11 oz) ready-rolled shortcrust pastry
1 egg, beaten

Coronation Chicken

/ Serves 4 / Ready in 30 minutes, plus cooling /

Mix the chicken, mild curry power, ground cinnamon, juice of ½ lemon, salt and a few grinds of pepper together in a large bowl.

Line the air fryer's grill plate with baking parchment. Add the chicken in a singer layer and spray with oil. Cook at 200°C (400°F) for 15 minutes, turning over halfway through cooking. Check it's cooked through – make a small cut and check to see if the fibres are set. Once finished cooking, remove the chicken from the basket and leave to cool to room temperature. You can use the refrigerator to speed up the process.

Meanwhile, in another large bowl, mix the mayonnaise with the yoghurt, mild curry powder, sultanas and mango chutney. Add the salt, a few grinds of pepper and stir until well combined.

Once the chicken has cooled, slice it, then add it to the curried mayo. Stir everything together so the chicken is well coated.

To make the green salad, toss the lettuce with the juice from the other half of lemon, the olive oil and the salt.

Serve the Coronation chicken on a sharing plate or bowl with a sprinkling of flaked almonds together with the green salad.

3 skinless, boneless chicken breasts, each halved lengthways
½ teaspoon mild curry powder
⅛ teaspoon ground cinnamon
1 lemon, halved
large pinch of salt
freshly ground black pepper
cooking oil spray
1 tablespoon flaked (slivered) almonds

FOR THE CURRIED MAYONNAISE
8 tablespoons mayonnaise
4 tablespoons Greek yoghurt
2 teaspoons mild curry powder
3 tablespoons sultanas (golden raisins)
4 tablespoons mango chutney
large pinch of salt

FOR THE GREEN SALAD
100 g (3½ oz) bag green lettuce
1 tablespoon extra virgin olive oil
pinch of salt

Chicken Meatballs

/ Serves 4 / Ready in 30 minutes /

In a large bowl, using your hands, mix the mince with the breadcrumbs, garlic, thyme, lemon zest, egg, 2 tablespoons of the Parmesan and salt until well combined. Shape the mixture into 20 meatballs, about the size of a ping-pong ball, and put onto a large plate or chopping board ready to cook. To make the shaping easier, have a small bowl of water to dip your hands into when the mixture becomes too sticky. Spray the meatballs all over with oil.

Line the air fryer's grill plate with baking parchment. Arrange the meatballs in a single layer on the parchment and cook at 200°C (400°F) for 14 minutes, turning over halfway through cooking.

Meanwhile, mix the mayonnaise with half of the juice of the zested lemon in a small bowl. Set aside.

Once the meatballs are cooked and golden, serve them with a sprinkling of the remaining Parmesan alongside the lemon mayo dipping sauce and a few toothpicks for guests to help themselves.

500 g (1 lb 2 oz) minced (ground) chicken (turkey mince works too)
2 tablespoons breadcrumbs, fresh or ready-made
2 garlic cloves, crushed
1 teaspoon dried thyme
zest and juice of 1 lemon
1 egg, beaten
3 tablespoons grated Parmesan
1 teaspoon salt
cooking oil spray
4 heaped tablespoons mayonnaise

Spinach, Chicken and Feta Pie

/ Serves 4 / Ready in 45 minutes, plus cooling /

Remove the grill plate from the air fryer's basket.

Add the chicken, onion, garlic, salt and cooking oil to the basket, stir together, then spread it out in an even layer. Cook at 200°C (400°F) for 7 minutes, stirring halfway through cooking.

Add the spinach and stir in for about 1 minute, or until the spinach starts to wilt. Cook at 200°C (400°F) for 4 minutes, stirring halfway through cooking.

Transfer the chicken and spinach mixture to a bowl and drain off any excess liquid, by pressing the mixture to remove as much liquid as possible. Leave to cool, refrigerating it to speed up the process.

Once cooled, drain any liquid that's formed. Stir in the cornflour, then add the feta and a few grinds of pepper.

Spray the cake tin (pan) with oil, then line it with the sheets of filo pastry, working with one sheet at a time and rotating to make a star that covers all sides of the tin. Gently press the pastry into the inside edges of the tin and spray each layer with oil, leaving the excess pastry hanging over the edge.

Add the chicken mixture to the tin, spreading it out evenly. Fold the overhanging pastry up and over the top of the pie, folding up one layer at a time. The pastry will crinkle and fold into itself, making an uneven pie lid. Spray all over with oil.

Put the grill plate back into the air fryer. Add the pie and cook at 180°C (350°F) for the first 5 minutes (check after 2 minutes of cooking and press down any folds that are blowing up using the back of a wooden spoon). Then reduce the temperature to 160°C (325°F) and cook for 17 minutes, or until the pastry is dark golden.

Leave the pie to rest for 10 minutes in the tin, then carefully remove it and serve.

2 skinless, boneless chicken breasts, cut into bite-size pieces
1 red onion, halved and thinly sliced
2 garlic cloves, crushed
pinch of salt
1 tablespoon cooking oil
200 g (7 oz) bag washed and ready-to-eat young spinach
1 teaspoon cornflour (cornstarch)
200 g (7 oz) feta cheese, crumbled
freshly ground black pepper
cooking oil spray
5 sheets of filo pastry (I used Jus Rol 26 x 44 cm/10½ x 17½ in)

You will need a 20 cm (8 in) loose-based cake tin (pan) and an air fryer with a basket large enough to fit it in (a 7–8 litre/1.5–1.8 gallon air fryer).

Chicken Summer Rolls

/ Makes 8 / Ready in 20 minutes /

Mix the chicken strips, sweet chilli sauce, coconut milk and salt together in a large bowl.

Line the air fryer's grill plate with baking parchment, then add the marinated chicken in a single. Cook at 200°C (400°F) for 10 minutes or until cooked through. Remove and leave to cool, refrigerating it to speed up the process.

Add the noodles to the lined grill plate (it's fine to use the same baking parchment the chicken was on). Spray with oil and cook at 200°C (400°F) for 3 minutes. Remove and set aside (it's okay if some of the noodles are crispy).

Slice the chicken into thin long strips. Lay out the other ingredients on a chopping board, then work on one summer roll at a time. Follow the packet's instructions on how to prep the wrappers. It will most likely say to dip each wrapper in a bowl of water for a few seconds to soften.

In the middle of a damp, soft wrapper, first lay two mint leaves (vibrant green-side down), then some noodles, followed by the chicken, carrot and finishing with the coriander. Repeat another seven times. Dampen your fingers and fold in the short ends first, then fold the end closest to you over the filling and keep rolling until sealed. Be gentle and dampen your fingers any time the wrapper starts to feel sticky.

For the dipping sauce, in a small serving bowl, stir the chopped peanuts into the sweet chilli sauce.

Serve your rolls with the peanut chilli sauce and enjoy.

1 skinless, boneless chicken breast, cut into 4 strips lengthways
1 tablespoon sweet chilli sauce
2 tablespoons coconut milk
pinch of salt
300 g (10½ oz) straight to wok vermicelli rice noodles (or use plain or Singapore-style)
cooking oil spray
8 rice paper spring roll wrappers (I used Blue Dragon's Vietnamese Spring Roll Wrappers)
16 mint leaves
1 carrot, cut into matchsticks
16 coriander (cilantro) leaves

FOR THE DIPPING SAUCE
1 heaped tablespoon roasted peanuts, chopped
4 tablespoons sweet chilli sauce

Chicken and Parmesan Arancini

/ Makes 8 / Ready in 30 minutes, plus chilling /

Using a fork, beat two of the eggs in a large bowl. Add the rice, Parmesan, butter, chicken, herbs, salt and a few grinds of pepper and mix together until evenly combined. Freeze for 15 minutes, or chill in the refrigerator for 30 minutes.

With clean, damp hands, shape the rice mixture into eight even-sized balls. Press a cube of mozzarella into each ball and reshape to cover the cheese.

In a shallow dish, combine the breadcrumbs with the salt. In another dish, lightly beat the remaining egg.

Dip each ball into the egg so that the ball is entirely covered, then roll in the seasoned breadcrumbs until coated. Add them to the air fryer's grill plate and spray all over with oil. Cook at 200°C (400°F) for 10 minutes until the tops are golden in colour.

Serve with a sprinkling of salt and your choice of dipping sauce, such as marinara or garlic aioli.

3 eggs
250 g (9 oz) pouch microwave long-grain rice, squeeze the pouch to break up the rice
60 g (2 oz) Parmesan, finely grated
2 tablespoons butter, softened
100 g (3½ oz) cooked chicken, finely chopped
½ teaspoon dried mixed herbs
1 teaspoon sea salt flakes, plus one pinch for serving
freshly ground black pepper
60 g (2 oz) mozzarella, cut into 8 cubes (I used Galbani Cucina Mozzarella Cheese)
80 g (2¾ oz) panko breadcrumbs
large pinch of salt
cooking oil spray
choice of dipping sauce, such as marinara sauce or garlic aioli, to serve

BAR SNACKS

Peri-Peri Chicken and Spicy Sweet Potato Fries

If you have a dual basket air fryer, then cook the chicken and fries at the same time. If not, then cook the fries after the chicken while the chicken is resting.

/ Serves 2 / Ready in 30 minutes if cooking immediately /

Mix the peri-peri seasoning, cooking oil and salt together in a small bowl. Using your hands, spread the marinade all over the chicken legs, getting into where you made the cuts. Place on a plate, cover, then put into the refrigerator. Leave to marinate for up to 24 hours, or you can cook straight away.

When ready to cook, place the legs, side by side and skin-side down, on the air fryer's grill plate. Cook at 200°C (400°F) for 22 minutes, turning the pieces over halfway through cooking. Once cooked through (test by cutting into them at the thickest part to see if the fibres are set), set them aside loosely covered in kitchen foil.

To make the fries, mix the smoked paprika, garlic powder and salt together in a small bowl. In a large bowl, mix the fries with the oil. Add the spice mix to the fries and stir well so every fry is coated in the spices.

Add the fries to the grill plate, spreading out in an even layer. Cook at 200°C (400°F) for 12 minutes, shaking the basket a few times during cooking.

For the lime mayo, mix the mayonnaise with the juice from half of the lime and the spring onion. Cut the other half of lime into wedges.

Serve the peri-peri chicken with the spicy fries, lime mayo dip and lime wedges on the side.

1 tablespoon dried peri-peri seasoning
1 tablespoon cooking oil
2 pinches of salt
2 chicken legs, skin on, make 3 small cuts in the skin to each

FOR THE FRIES
½ teaspoon smoked paprika
½ teaspoon garlic powder
2 pinches of salt
2 sweet potatoes, peeled and cut into 1 cm (½ in) fries
1 tablespoon cooking oil

FOR THE LIME MAYO DIP
4 tablespoons mayonnaise
1 lime, halved
1 spring onion (scallion), finely chopped

BBQ Chicken Pizzette

/ Serves 1 / Takes 15 minutes /

Mix 1 tablespoon of the BBQ sauce and the sliced chicken together in a large bowl.

Spread the remaining BBQ sauce over the naan. Sprinkle over the cheese, then add the chicken, onion and jalapeños on top.

Using two hands, carefully lift the pizzette and place it on the air fryer's grill plate. Spray generously with oil and cook at 200°C (400°F) for 6 minutes, or until the cheese is melted.

Enjoy with your favourite pizza dipping sauce – I like ranch or garlic mayo.

3 tablespoons BBQ sauce (I used Sauce Shop Honey and Chipotle BBQ Sauce)
1 cooked skinless, boneless chicken breast, sliced
1 plain naan
handful of grated mozzarella
¼ small red onion, finely sliced
1 tablespoon pickled jalapeño pepper slices
cooking oil spray
pizza dipping sauce of choice, to serve

Cornish Pasties

/ Makes 3 pasties / Ready in 30 minutes /

Mix the mustard and Marmite together in a large bowl to a thick paste. Add the onion, carrot, potato, cheese and chicken and mix everything together really well.

On a lightly floured work surface, roll out the pastry large enough to cut out about 3 x 18 cm (7 in) rounds (use a side dish as a template). You might need to stamp out two, then re-roll the pastry cut-offs to get the third round. If so, then refrigerate the other two rounds until you are ready to assemble.

Divide the chicken mixture evenly between each pastry round, adding the filling down the centre of each. Brush the edges with a little of the beaten egg, then bring up the sides to meet over the filling. Press the edges firmly together to seal, then crimp the edges using your fingers. To crimp, push your forefinger on your left hand between your forefinger and thumb on your right hand to get the right effect. Brush all over with more egg to glaze the pasties.

Line the grill fryer's plate with baking parchment, then sit the pasties side by side, not touching, on it. You may have to cook in batches depending on the size of your air fryer. Cook at 200°C (400°F) for 5 minutes, then reduce the temperature to 180°C (350°F) and cook for a further 10 minutes.

Using a spatula or two forks, turn the pasties on their sides so the bottoms can finish cooking. Cook at 180°C (350°F) for a further 5 minutes.

Leave the pasties to stand for 5 minutes, then serve hot or at room temperature.

2 teaspoons Dijon mustard
1 teaspoon Marmite or yeast extract
1 onion, grated
1 medium carrot, grated
1 potato, grated
50 g (1¾ oz) Cheddar, grated
1 skinless, boneless chicken breast, cut into small cubes
plain (all-purpose) flour, for dusting
500 g (1 lb 2 oz) ready-made shortcrust pastry
1 egg, beaten

Buffalo Hot Wings

/ Serves 2 / Ready in 30 minutes /

In North America, wings are served cut in half. You don't have to do this but for real Buffalo wings, use a sharp large kitchen knife to cut down where the joint is to separate the wing into two pieces.

Pat the wings dry with paper towels. In a large bowl, mix the smoked paprika with the garlic powder, baking powder and salt. Add the wings and coat all over.

Spray the air fryer's grill plate with oil. Add the wings and cook at 200°C (400°F) for 25 minutes, turning the wings over a couple of times during cooking.

Meanwhile, in a large bowl, use a balloon whisk to mix the hot sauce with the melted butter and ketchup.

To make the dip, mix the sour cream, mayonnaise, blue cheese and vinegar together in a small bowl.

Once the wings are cooked and golden, add them to the bowl with the sauce. Mix everything together so that every wing is well coated in hot sauce.

Serve the wings alongside the crudités, blue cheese dip and lots of napkins.

photograph on previous page

750 g (1 lb 10 oz) chicken wings, cut the tips off the wings if not already done
1 teaspoon smoked paprika
¼ teaspoon garlic powder or granules
1 teaspoon baking powder
large pinch of salt
cooking oil spray

FOR THE HOT SAUCE
100 ml (3½ fl oz/scant ½ cup) hot sauce (I used Frank's Red Hot)
25 g (1 oz) butter, melted
2 tablespoons tomato ketchup

FOR THE BLUE CHEESE DIP
4 tablespoons sour cream
1 tablespoon mayonnaise
3 tablespoons crumbled blue cheese
1 teaspoon white wine vinegar

FOR THE CRUDITÉS
1 carrot, cut into sticks
1 celery stalk, cut into sticks

Chicken Caesar Salad

/ Serves 1 / Ready in 20 minutes /

To make the croutons, spray one side of the bread with oil. Sprinkle over a pinch of oregano and a pinch of salt, turn over and repeat. Cut the seasoned bread into bite-size squares.

Lay the pieces in a singer layer on the air fryer's grill plate and cook at 200°C (400°F) for 3 minutes until lightly toasted and starting to colour. Set aside to cool.

For the dressing, in a bowl, mix the mayonnaise with the crushed garlic, lemon zest, the juice from half of the lemon, the mustard, Parmesan, salt and a few grinds of pepper.

Line the air fryer's basket with baking parchment (no need to clean it from the croutons). Add the chicken in a single layer. Spray the chicken with oil, then spoon over 2 tablespoons of the Caesar dressing. Cook at 200°C (400°F) for 8 minutes. Add the capers around the chicken and cook for a further 3 minutes.

Add the lettuce to a serving plate or bowl and spoon over the remaining dressing. Top with the chicken, capers and croutons, and enjoy.

1 slice of crusty bread
cooking oil spray
2 pinches of dried oregano
2 pinches of salt

FOR THE DRESSING
2 tablespoons mayonnaise
½ garlic clove, crushed
zest of 1 lemon, then halved
1 teaspoon Dijon mustard
2 tablespoons finely grated
  Parmesan
pinch of salt
freshly ground black pepper

FOR THE CHICKEN
1 skinless, boneless chicken
  breast, sliced
1 tablespoon capers
1 baby gem lettuce head, leaves
  separated and roughly chopped

Spring Rolls

Add the bean sprouts, carrot, spring onions, garlic, ginger, chicken, sesame oil, Shaoxing rice wine and soy sauce to a large bowl and mix everything together well.

On a dinner plate, divide the chicken mixture out into six small piles. Working with one roll at a time, add one-sixth of the mixture to the bottom quarter of the first sheet of pastry and spread to about 11 cm (4¼ in) wide. Spray the oil around the edges, then fold in the left and right sides over the filling. Spray the pastry again, then gently but tightly roll all the way up. Repeat with the remaining five rolls. It may look like too small an amount of filling for the size of the pastry but you want lots of layers when using filo.

Spray the air fryer's grill plate with oil. Add the rolls in a single layer and spray the rolls generously with oil. Cook at 190°C (375°F) for 12 minutes, turning the rolls over halfway through cooking and spraying them again.

Meanwhile, to make the dipping sauce, in a small bowl, mix the soy sauce with the honey until completely combined.

Serve the spring rolls with the dipping sauce and enjoy.

150 g (5½ oz/1⅔ cups) bean sprouts
1 carrot, grated
2 spring onions (scallions), thinly sliced
1 garlic clove, finely chopped
3 cm (1¼ in) piece of fresh ginger, peeled and finely chopped
1 skinless, boneless chicken breast, finely chopped
1 teaspoon sesame oil
½ teaspoon Shaoxing rice wine or any wine vinegar
1 tablespoon dark soy sauce
6 sheets of filo pastry
cooking oil spray

FOR THE DIPPING SAUCE
2 tablespoons dark soy sauce
2 tablespoons runny honey

Coconut Chicken Skewers

/ Makes 4 skewers / Ready in 30 minutes /

Mix the sweet chilli sauce, a pinch of salt and a few grinds of pepper together in a large bowl. Add the chicken and turn to coat all over.

Spread the coconut out on a large plate and sprinkle with ½ teaspoon salt. Coat the chicken in the salted coconut, then thread the strips onto four metal or wooden skewers. Spray generously with oil.

Lay the skewers on the air fryer's grill plate or if you have an air fryer rack for skewers, then use that and cook at 200°C (400°F) for 12 minutes, turning the skewers over halfway through cooking. The coconut will become quite dark in colour but that's okay, it adds to the flavour. If they are becoming too charred for your liking then turn the heat down to 180°C (350°F) and cook for a few minutes longer. Check the chicken is cooked through by cutting into a thick part of the meat and checking to see if the fibres are set.

Serve with sweet chilli sauce and lime wedges.

4 tablespoons sweet chilli sauce
salt and freshly ground black pepper
2 skinless, boneless chicken breasts, sliced into strips about 1 cm (½ in) thick
50 g (1¾ oz/½ cup) desiccated (dried shredded) coconut
cooking oil spray

TO SERVE
sweet chilli sauce
1 lime, cut into wedges

You can use metal or wooden skewers but they must fit inside your air fryer's basket. If using wooden skewers, then break them to the size needed and soak in a bowl of cold water for at least 5 minutes.

Club Sandwich

/ Serves 2 / Ready in 30 minutes /

In batches, lay the bread slices on the air fryer's grill plate in a single layer and cook at 200°C (400°F) for 3–4 minutes, turning over halfway through cooking. They should be only lightly toasted. Remove and leave to cool.

Arrange the slices of bacon on the air fryer's grill plate in a single layer. You may have to do this in batches depending on the size of your air fryer. Cook at 200°C (400°F) for 6 minutes. Transfer the bacon to paper towels to drain any excess fat. There is no need to clean the air fryer before the chicken is added.

Spray the chicken breasts all over with oil, then season with the salt and a few grinds of pepper. Place on the grill plate and cook at 200°C (400°F) for 16 minutes. Leave the chicken to rest for 5 minutes, then remove from the air fryer and thinly slice it.

To assemble, spread the mayonnaise thickly on two slices of toast. Spread butter on the other four slices. First, add a layer of tomato slices on top of the mayo slices of toast, then two slices of bacon on top of the tomatoes (four in total), then a layer of chicken slices, followed by lettuce. Add two slices of the buttered toast, then begin your second layer of filling in each sandwich. Add any tomato that is left, the remaining bacon, followed by the rest of the chicken and lettuce. Top with the final slices of buttered toast, buttered-side down.

Using a large bread knife, cut the sandwiches diagonally into triangles. Use cocktail sticks (toothpicks) to help them hold together and serve with crisps and pickles.

6 slices of white bread
6 slices of streaky bacon
2 skinless, boneless chicken breasts
cooking oil spray
pinch of salt
freshly ground black pepper
3 tablespoons mayonnaise
butter, softened
1 large or 4 vine tomatoes, sliced
5–8 crunchy green lettuce leaves (I used little gem lettuce)

TO SERVE
crisps (chips)
pickle spears

Chicken, Leek and Mushroom Pie

/ Serves 1 / Ready in 20 minutes /

Remove the air fryer's grill plate. Add the oil, leek and mushrooms to the basket and stir. Cook at 200°C (400°F) for 8 minutes, stirring halfway through cooking.

Add the chicken, garlic, salt, a few grinds of pepper and stir. Cook at 200°C (400°F) for 6 minutes, stirring halfway through cooking.

Add the crème fraîche, hot water and stock cube and stir everything together until the stock cube has dissolved. Pour the cooked mixture into the pie dish and refrigerate for 10 minutes.

Meanwhile, clean the air fryer's basket.

Once the chicken mixture has cooled to room temperature, roll out the pastry and lift on top of the pie dish. Using a sharp knife, cut off the overhanging pastry, then using your fingers or a fork, crimp the edges to seal the pastry to the dish. Brush the pastry with the beaten egg, then using the tip of a knife, make a small hole in the centre of the pie to release the steam.

Carefully lift the pie into the air fryer's basket and cook at 180°C (350°F) for 15 minutes, or until the pastry is golden and the filling is piping hot.

Leave to stand for a few minutes, then dig in!

You will need a small pie dish that fits into your air fryer's basket. I used a 14.5 x 19.5 cm (5¾ x 8 in) pie dish.

1 tablespoon cooking oil
1 leek, finely sliced
5 chestnut mushrooms, sliced
1 skinless, boneless chicken breast, cut into bite-size pieces
1 garlic clove, crushed
pinch of salt
freshly ground black pepper
4 tablespoons crème fraîche
3 tablespoons hot water
½ chicken stock cube, crumbled
½ x 320 g (11 oz) ready-rolled puff pastry sheet
1 egg, beaten

Chicken and Black Bean Nachos

/ Serves 4 / Ready in 20 minutes /

Mix the chicken, black beans, smoked paprika, cumin seeds, salt and oil together in a large bowl.

Line the air fryer's grill plate with baking parchment. Add the chicken mixture and spread out evenly. Cook at 200°C (400°F) for 8 minutes, stirring halfway through cooking.

Pour the chicken mixture into a clean bowl and stir in any juices left in the basket with the mayonnaise and hot sauce.

Remove the used baking parchment from the grill plate and reline it with baking parchment that comes 4 cm (1½ in) up on each side.

Add half of the tortilla chips to the basket. Spoon over half of the chicken mix, half of the cheese, half of the jalapeños, half of the tomato and half of the spring onions. Repeat the layers one more time. Cook at 180°C (350°F) for 2–4 minutes until the cheese has melted.

For the guacamole, in a bowl, mix the smashed avocado with the lime juice and salt.

Remove the nachos by lifting out the baking parchment with the nachos inside. You may need a friend to grab two corners of the paper as well.

Serve in the paper on a chopping board or platter, scattered with the coriander and the guacamole on the side.

2–3 skinless, boneless chicken thighs, cut into small bite-size pieces
400 g (14 oz) tin black beans, drained and rinsed
2 teaspoons smoked paprika
1 teaspoon cumin seeds
½ teaspoon salt
2 teaspoons cooking oil
2 tablespoons mayonnaise
2 teaspoons hot sauce
1 bag (about 170 g/6 oz) lightly salted tortilla chips
150 g (5½ oz) grated mozzarella or mild Cheddar
2 tablespoons pickled jalapeño pepper slices
1 tomato, chopped
2 spring onions (scallions), chopped
handful of coriander (cilantro) leaves, to serve

FOR THE GUACAMOLE
1 avocado, peeled, pitted and smashed
juice of 1 lime
pinch of salt

Parmesan Garlic Tenders with Smoky Ketchup

/ Serves 2 as a main or 4 as a snack / Ready in 30 minutes /

Add the beaten egg to a shallow bowl, then add the chicken strips. Turn each strip over a few times to completely coat in the egg.

In a large bowl, mix the Parmesan with the garlic, salt and a few grinds of black pepper. Add the chicken, one strip at a time, and heavily coat all over. Transfer the finished strips to a clean plate or chopping board.

Spray the air fryer's grill plate with oil. Add the chicken tenders in a single layer and spray all over with oil. Cook at 200°C (400°F) for 12 minutes. Using two forks, turn the tenders over and cook for a further 2 minutes.

Meanwhile, in a small serving bowl, mix the ketchup with the paprika.

Serve the tenders, golden-side up, with the smoky dip on the side and enjoy.

1 egg, beaten
2 skinless, boneless chicken breasts, each cut lengthways into 4 strips
100 g (3½ oz) Parmesan, finely grated
1 teaspoon garlic powder or granules
pinch of salt
freshly ground black pepper
cooking oil spray

FOR THE DIP
2 tablespoons tomato ketchup
1 teaspoon smoked paprika

Chorizo and Chicken Burgers with Swiss Cheese

/ Serves 4 / Ready in 30 minutes /

Using your hands, combine the mince with the chorizo, smoked paprika, parsley, salt and a few grinds of pepper in a large bowl. Shape the mixture into four burger patties slightly wider than the burger buns. Press your thumb into the middle of the patties to make an indentation. This helps the patties keep their shape during cooking.

Spray the patties with oil and lay on the air fryer's grill plate in a single layer. Cook at 200°C (400°F) for 10 minutes. Flip the patties over and cook for a further 5 minutes. Make a small cut into the centre of the patty to check the mince is cooked through, the fibres are set and the centre is piping hot.

Once done, leave the burgers in the air fryer and add a slice of cheese to each. Close the air fryer and allow the cheese to melt for 1 minute, with the air fryer off.

Serve the burgers in the buns with red onion, tomato and lettuce. Have your condiments ready for your guests to help themselves. I like ketchup and mustard with these.

500 g (1 lb 2 oz) minced (ground) chicken (turkey mince can be used too)
85 g (3 oz) raw chorizo sausage, meat removed from the casings (I used Unearthered Mini Cooking Chorizo Sausages)
½ teaspoon smoked paprika
handful of fresh parsley, chopped
½ teaspoon salt
freshly ground black pepper
cooking oil spray
4 slices Emmental cheese
4 burger buns, halved
1 small red onion, sliced
1 large tomato, sliced
1 baby gem lettuce, thinly sliced
condiments of choice, to serve

Index

honey: dipping sauce 125
   honey garlic drumsticks 89
   hot honey chicken 44
hot sauce: buffalo hot wings 122
   chicken and black bean nachos 132
   chicken bean burritos 74
   hot honey chicken 44

ingredients 10

kebabs *see* skewers

leeks: chicken, leek and mushroom pie 130
lemon chicken with rice 80
lettuce: chicken Caesar salad 123
   chorizo and chicken burgers 136
   club sandwich 128
   crispy sesame chicken salad 28
   green salad 104
limes: guacamole 132
   lime mayo dip 114
   peanut dipping sauce 90
liners 9

mayonnaise: bacon chicken burger 78
   bang bang chicken 70
   blue cheese dip 122
   chicken and black bean nachos 132
   chicken Caesar salad 123
   chicken meatballs 105
   club sandwich 128
   coronation chicken 104
   lime mayo dip 114
   pesto chicken crostini 96
   shawarma wraps 84
meatballs, chicken 105
Mediterranean chicken skewers 99
mint: chicken summer rolls 108
   mint yoghurt dip 99
   raita 69
mushrooms: chicken and mushroom
     stroganoff 42
   chicken, leek and mushroom pie 130
   chicken supreme with new potatoes 49

nachos, chicken and black bean 132

noodles: chicken chow mein 64
   chicken summer rolls 108
nori: teriyaki sushi rolls 24
nuggets, chicken 83

oil, cooking spray 9–10
olives: chicken and chorizo empanadas 103
   stuffed peppers 22
omelette, tarragon chicken 15
onions: bacon chicken burger 78
   chicken fried rice 100
   Cornish pasties 118
   roast dinner 60
   spinach, chicken and feta pie 106
   see also spring onions
orange chicken, avocado and pine nut
     wrap 26

paella: chicken, chorizo and prawn 50
Parmesan garlic tenders 135
pasties, Cornish 118
pastries: Chinese chicken sausage rolls 92
     spring rolls 125
   see also pies; tarts
peanut butter: peanut dipping sauce 90
peanuts: dipping sauce 108
peas: chicken pot pie 58
peppers (bell): chicken, chorizo and prawn
     paella 50
   chicken chow mein 64
   Mediterranean chicken skewers 99
   stuffed peppers 22
peri-peri chicken 114
pesto chicken crostini 96
pies: chicken and chorizo empanadas 103
   chicken, leek and mushroom pie 130
   chicken pot pie 58
   Cornish pasties 118
   spinach, chicken and feta pie 106
   see also pastries; tarts
pine nuts: orange chicken, avocado and pine
     nut wrap 26
   pesto 96
pistachio nuts: chicken, apricot and pistachio
     tagine 54
pizzette, BBQ chicken 117

About the Author

Kate Calder is a trained chef, writer, recipe tester and food stylist with more than a decade's worth of experience in the kitchens of *BBC Good Food*, *Olive* and *Good Housekeeping* magazines. She's written and styled for many publications but equally enjoys testing other chef's recipes at home and feeding her friends & neighbours. This is her third cookbook, she is also the author of *3 Ingredient Cocktails* and *Happiness in a Mug Cake*. Hailing from Toronto, Canada, but now based in London with her young family, Kate's passion for food led her away from her previous career in the film industry but she continues to watch an unhealthy amount of film and TV.

Acknowledgements

A massive thank you to the team behind this book. Issy, for your inspiration and guidance, Nikki and Hannah, for your beautiful design and props, Katy for your incredible cooking and styling skills, and Ant, for your gorgeous photography.

Lastly, thank you to Ben, Sonny and Bo for being the best family I could ever wish for (and for eating a lot of chicken).

Quadrille, Penguin Random House UK,
One Embassy Gardens, 8 Viaduct Gardens,
London SW11 7BW

Quadrille Publishing Limited is part of the
Penguin Random House group of companies
whose addresses can be found at global.
penguinrandomhouse.com

Published by Quadrille in 2025

www.penguin.co.uk

A CIP catalogue record for this book is
available from the British Library

ISBN 978-178488-803-9

10 9 8 7 6 5 4 3 2 1

Publishing Director: Kajal Mistry

Commissioning Editor: Isabel Gonzalez-
Prendergast

Designer and Art Director: Nikki Ellis

Photographer: Anthony Duncan

Props Stylist: Hannah Wilkinson

Food Stylist: Katy Greenwood

Production Manager: Sabeena Atchia

Colour reproduction by p2d

Printed in China by RR Donnelley Asia Printing
Solution Limited

The authorised representative in the
EEA is Penguin Random House Ireland,
Morrison Chambers, 32 Nassau Street,
Dublin D02 YH68.

Penguin Random House is committed
to a sustainable future for our business,
our readers and our planet. This book is
made from Forest Stewardship Council®
certified paper.